sidebyside LEARNING

Exemplary Literacy Practices for English Language Learners and English Speakers in the Mainstream Classroom

Carole Edelsky, Karen Smith, and Christian Faltis

■SCHOLASTIC

New York • Toronto • London • Auckland • Sydney
Mexico City • New Delhi • Hong Kong • Buenos Aires

Credits

Figures 1.1, 1.2, 1.3, the *Writing to Learn chart*, and the *BKWLQ* chart from
Yellow Brick Roads: Shared and Guided Paths to Independent Reading 4–12
by Janet Allen, copyright © 2000, reprinted with permission of Stenhouse Publishers.

. . . .

Cover design by Jay Namerow

Interior design by Sydney Wright

Cover photograph by Maria Lilja

Interior photographs by Karen Smith

Acquiring Editor: Lois Bridges

Production Editor: Erin K.L. Grelak

DVD Producer: Jane Buchbinder

Copy Editor: Chris Borris

ISBN-13: 978-0-545-03516-3

ISBN-10: 0-545-03516-3

For Casey, Ernestina, and Rebecca, teachers extraordinaire

Contents

Introduction

C'mon in. No need to tiptoe. These fifth graders are so engrossed in a unit on motion and design that they'll hardly notice you. The same goes for their teacher. Ms. Aragón is concentrating on some "kids' talk" in a small group so she can make the speakers feel smart and at the same time push their thinking. That foursome spread out on the floor near the beanbag chairs? Two are just learning English. All four are trying to make their Lego-looking vehicle move ten feet by means of wound-up rubber bands. And the three kids at that table are coaxing their vehicle to move up a ramp and stop exactly at the top. The boy with the red shirt—the one reading and rereading the instructions printed in English on what their vehicle is supposed to do—entered the United States just this year. This is that trio's third attempt to get their vehicle to "meet the challenge"—the specifications—laid out in the packaged science program. The four girls at the table consulting a chart they wrote earlier in the unit are switching between English and Spanish as they argue about the kind of force that will best push the vehicle they are to design. Even though two of them are not very proficient in English, all can work together on this task.

English learners and English speakers learning side by side

How is it that in this classroom the English learners and the English speakers are learning together, side by side? How is it that the focus is on interesting content that kids can sink their teeth into even if they aren't proficient in English? How is it that these students don't groan at the prospect of writing but instead seem ever poised to write and later reread their ideas? How does it happen that no one is "off task" and no one is misbehaving? After all, what typically happens when English learners and English speakers are in the same classroom is more like the following:

In a third-grade classroom in a huge Midwestern city, 15 students are sitting in a semi-circle on the floor around the teacher. They're listening with rapt attention to her read *The Tale of Despereaux* (2003) by Kate DiCamillo. Ten others are sitting with an instructional aide at two tables pushed together. The aide is alternately drilling them on initial and final consonants and prodding them to pay attention. The kids treated to the engrossing story are English speakers. Those consigned to the content-less drill are English learners. The teacher and the aide believe they are helping the English learners with basics in English literacy so that some day they can join the others for read-aloud time.

Students reading and writing English as well as learning about the content of the study

Another example, this one from a small school in a smaller city in the Southwest. Here, the fourth-grade students are paired up, one English learner and one English speaker in each pair. The English speaker is supposed to act as a tutor, helping the other complete a worksheet on synonyms. Most of those being helped—and many of the helpers, too—are having trouble identifying the words on the worksheet, but the teacher believes working in pairs helps everyone. He says, "You learn a lot by teaching someone else." And it helps the teacher, too, because "I don't know how else I can have them all working on the same lesson."

In the fifth-grade class next door, the teacher doesn't try to give both English learners and English speakers the same assignments. "They [the English learners] can't understand English," he argues, the other teachers on the upper-grade team nodding their agreement. "What would be the point?" So while the English speakers write stories, the English learners do a page of arithmetic problems because "multiplication is the same no matter what language the kids speak." When the English learners finish the arithmetic problems, they can draw on the back of their papers. And they do. They produce intricate designs on the backs but, alas, complete few problems on the fronts.

These examples are more typical of what teachers do when they are unprepared for a class of both English learners and English speakers. They segregate the students by language and have the English learners work on small bits of (usually written) English while the English speakers do something more interesting, or they give the English learners lessons that don't depend on English, or they turn the English speakers into tutors so all can work on the same "skill."

The trouble is that these currently common accommodations don't serve anyone very well. They ensure that English learners see themselves as—and in fact become—poor students, bored and disengaged. They guarantee that English speakers get confirmation of popular prejudices, seeing themselves as superior to English learners, whose very presence holds everyone else back. And they erode teachers' self-confidence when, while wrestling with doubts in the middle of the night, they hear their own voices telling them, "You really aren't reaching all your students."

When did such practices become commonplace? Not so long ago, it seemed that in most classrooms, "regular" teachers taught "regular" English-speaking kids. But then, overnight, something happened. On Monday, all the kids in "regular" classrooms had been English speakers. On Tuesday, half were English learners.

Students creating a plan for their inquiry project

Of course, classrooms, kids, and teachers were never "regular." And the presence of large numbers of English learners in large numbers of classrooms throughout the United States did not happen overnight. But whether overnight or gradually, the fact is there were 900,000 English learners in U.S. classrooms in 1990. By 2005, there were more than three million. In Arizona alone, nearly half of the 250,000 K–12 students are designated as English learners. Most are from Spanish-speaking countries, but that doesn't mean they all speak Spanish. Many speak indigenous languages such as Náhuatl, Maya, Mixteco, or Otomí. Other English learners come from Indochina (Vietnam, Laos, Cambodia), Haiti, Russia, North Africa, and the Middle East. Some have been attending school for about as long as their age-mates in the U.S. But others may have gone to school only sporadically. (How can a child go to school if his family depends on him to work in the fields or if she is fleeing her homeland?)

What happened to create this change? Increased immigration, for one thing. For another, decreased long-term programs offering language support. In some states, ballot propositions all but killed bilingual education. In others, budget and policy decisions put an end to self-contained English as a Second Language (ESL) classrooms. The net effect is that the "regulars" (regular teachers, regular students) who hardly ever saw the English learners "hidden" in bilingual and ESL classrooms now see them. Every day. All day. English learners are now sitting next to "regular" English speakers, waiting to be taught by "regular" teachers—by you.

A teacher accommodating English learners

If you're reading this right now, chances are you never expected to be teaching English learners. And you didn't get much, or any, preparation in second-language pedagogy. No surprise. If you don't have professional preparation for teaching English learners, you aren't prepared to teach English learners. After all, teachers used to do several years of graduate work to qualify for teaching English as a second language. Now, all of a sudden, a couple of weekend courses are supposed to suffice. As for knowing how to teach a class of English learners and English speakers together—newcomers who can't respond to "What's your name?" sitting next to bilingual kids who translate for their parents, who sit next to kids whose entire lives are conducted in English—where were you supposed to get such preparation? It wasn't (and mostly still isn't) part of "regular" teacher preparation programs. It's rarely even part of ESL graduate work. And adapting instruction to a huge range of English abilities isn't a major focus of most instructional materials.

You know the adjustments you've already made haven't been very successful. You also know you want to be the best teacher you can be for all your students, not just for those who speak English. But how? Our answer: *through inquiry-based curriculum* (including the parts of the curriculum that are offered on the spur of the moment).

Now we're not oblivious to current conditions in schools. We know you're under increasing pressure to prep kids for mandated tests. We know you're required to use particular materials and to stick to particular daily schedules. But even in schools with such requirements, every single minute is not restricted. And those moments of leeway—sometimes just the transition times or maybe an hour in the day, or a day of the week, or a subject area or a topic—can be used in ways that hook English learners as well as English speakers. When you infuse your curriculum—both the planned and the unplanned curriculum—with inquiry, you get more benefit than "merely" engaging learners. Inquiry elements, as we describe in this book and as shown on the DVD, support kids in learning new ways of talking, reading, and writing in English as well as in learning the content their inquiry is about.

We are fortunate to know three teachers (Ernestina Aragón and Rebecca Osorio, featured in the DVD), and Casey Bilger (featured in the Extra Clips), who are willing to show strangers (you) a way of working that is still somewhat new to them. We are not only grateful to them; we are completely awestruck by their courage! Nor are we working within our own comfort zones. The inquiry study on the Motion and Design unit we show on the DVD with Ernestina and Rebecca happened to be in a content area in which none of us is expert. But we think our fumbles and successes might look more like reality, and might help you be more willing to try some of our suggestions.

The DVD and book are meant to be used together. The DVD shows the inquiry-based adaptations Ernestina and Rebecca made to a required unit in a mandated commercial program. These are elements that you, too, can use for improving the quality of any topic of study and any window of time. They will enhance the literacy and language learning of all your students. The Extra Clips with Casey are for additional viewing and discussion.

We hope this set—the book and DVD—helps you become your best professional self for *all* your students, side by side, learning together.

Viewing Guide for the
Side-by-Side Learning DVD

The following guide provides some general advice for viewing the accompanying DVD, which showcases a Motion and Design inquiry project. The students explored physics concepts related to motion and applied their new understandings to designing a vehicle. Our intention is to help you pull as much learning out of the experience as possible. In order to do so, plan a time to watch the DVD with colleagues. Research— as well as our own experience—indicates that professional study groups create the best conditions for helping teachers learn. This DVD is for you because it focuses on teachers rather than students. It shines a spotlight on adaptations you might make in your own teaching. To enhance your own learning, watch the DVD all the way through to grasp our approach to side-by-side learning. Then watch it again (and again, as needed) for specific teaching opportunities. Each time you view it, look at it through one of the following lenses for thinking about side-by-side teaching and learning: 1) inquiry-based curriculum; 2) support for second language learning; or 3) support for literacy learning. **Please note:** The DVD reflects a case study of two classrooms engaged in side-by-side learning rather than a complete explanation of the inquiry process.

1) Lens for Viewing: Inquiry-Based Curriculum

Open-ended-ness

Inquiry-based curriculum is loaded with open-ended experiences. To Ernestina and Rebecca, *open-ended* meant experiences had no pre-set answers; students contributed their own knowledge to the content; teachers planned lots of opportunities for students to talk with peers and hear others' ideas; and teachers set "hooks" so students would dig deeply into the content.

- ❑ What does *open-ended* mean to you?

- ❑ How could you make what you're doing now more *open-ended*?

Experiential Learning

Ernestina and Rebecca wanted students to participate in experiences, not just one-time activities. *Experiences* include trial and error work. They rely on what students already know while inviting them to learn more. They prod students to raise questions about big ideas and pursue answers to these questions.

- ❑ Talk about a time when you engaged in learning through experience yourself.

- ❑ Discuss ways you could make some aspect of your curriculum include more experiential engagements for students.

Components of Inquiry

The DVD highlights four components of inquiry-based learning: building background knowledge, foregrounding students' own questions, focusing the study, and making a final presentation. Each of these provides fertile opportunities for side-by-side learning.

Building Background Knowledge

❑ Discuss ways Ernestina and Rebecca access their students' *background knowledge*.

❑ How are they getting their students to *build their background knowledge* as they further investigate the topic of motion and design?

Foregrounding Students' Questions

❑ Discuss some ways and formats that Ernestina and Rebecca put *students' questions* at the center of the work.

Creating a Final Project (which includes focusing the study)

Ernestina's and Rebecca's classes *created a final project* by helping their students to *focus their studies*—that is, by using what they observed and wondered about to determine the design of their vehicle.

❑ What evidence do you see that students are using what they've generated to *focus their efforts to design a final project* (a vehicle) that meets certain specifications?

Presenting New Knowledge

Presenting new knowledge solidifies learning. Rebecca and Ernestina helped students make the processes they went through explicit; they elicited new vocabulary; they helped students plan a variety of charts; and they ensured that all students participated.

❑ Where do you see evidence that the teachers' efforts paid off?

2) Lens for Viewing: Support for Second Language Learning

Ernestina and Rebecca adapted their teaching to provided support for their English language learners with language support, routines, demonstrations, and deliberate grouping. On the DVD, these adaptations are woven together—e.g., language support such as gesturing during a demonstration.

Language Support

Teachers have to be deliberate about language support—speaking more slowly, repeating, paraphrasing, emphasizing certain words, pointing to what they're reading from the board, exaggerating gestures, using objects, offering quick translations, etc. Good examples of language support (the use of gestures and visuals) begin 55 seconds after the start of the section called "Building Background," when Ernestina is summarizing what students learned about force.

Routines

Routines make classroom life run smoothly and cue English learners on what to do and what to say. They also require considerable practice. Each aspect has to be explicitly taught. For example, in

Think-Pair-Share, Ernestina and Rebecca had to carefully teach students to turn their bodies, look at each other, take turns, respond to what each other says, and stay on the topic. The Think-Pair-Share routine starts at 4:45. The Take Time to Think routine follows 30 seconds later.

Demonstrations

In this DVD, we focus on demonstrations that Rebecca and Ernestina intentionally created to help students do particular tasks or use particular formats. A demonstration on filling out a chart using a large version of that graphic organizer starts at 6:15.

Groupings

In grouping students, Rebecca and Ernestina considered who would get along with whom, whose temperament would be suitable for new English learners (e.g., who would be patient, who would refrain from making fun of a strong accent), and who would contribute to a "mix" of abilities in language and content. Evidence that students have been grouped deliberately begins at 7:30.

It may be helpful to stop the DVD after the first seven to eight minutes to talk about the four adaptations, which were made to support the learning of English. Then watch the rest of the DVD for evidence of these four strategies of adaptation for English learners.

❑ What additional **language support** could you use to help your English learners?

❑ How did **routines** expedite, enhance, or support this unit?

❑ How do these **demonstrations** designed to support English learners also help students who are fluent English speakers?

❑ Given your own population of students, what criteria for *grouping* do you need to consider?

3) Lens for Viewing: Support for Learning Literacy

Ernestina and Rebecca built in many opportunities for reading and writing as part of their work to design a vehicle. For instance, they had students write down their observations during experiments. The students on the DVD take for granted that they'll read and write as part of their work. They don't groan; it's no big deal; they just do it.

❑ In what other ways did students *read and write* as part of their work? How might the students have benefited from each of these literacy experiences?

❑ How do you think Ernestina and Rebecca taught them to just assume they'll *read and write* and to do it willingly?

❑ What routine formats helped students know what to *write*?

❑ Discuss how various social arrangements helped students concentrate on learning.

We hope that as you watch this DVD and talk with colleagues about it, you'll learn new ways to make your curriculum more open-ended, to engage students in experiential learning, and to adapt your teaching so it supports deep content learning while it promotes the learning of English and of literacy.

CHAPTER 1

Inquiry-Based Curriculum

. . . in true inquiry we often dedicate more time to figuring out and revising our questions than seeking "answers." In classrooms and learning contexts in which our students are invited to be inquirers, learning begins with what students know. Students are given the time, tools, and resources they need to generate questions. Inquiry questions are genuine—they're not questions students are *supposed* to ask or angled toward predetermined outcomes learners *should* discover. Inquirers explore issues, try out and reflect on new insights and understanding, in safe spaces; they're not always expected to *get it right*.

Katie Van Sluys,
What If and Why: Literacy Invitations for Multilingual Classrooms

Were you wondering when we'd finally explain what we mean by *inquiry-based curriculum*? At last! We begin right here—and we spell it out throughout this entire chapter.

At the heart of an inquiry-based curriculum is students' desire to know and to figure out "stuff." What appeals to us about an inquiry-based curriculum is that it grows out of a learning theory of how very young children construct understandings of their world. We all have watched toddlers being attracted to what is bright and noisy and unknown. We have seen them approach these objects or events with curiosity and resourcefulness—often tasting, smelling, and handling objects or closely observing events, deliberately trying to make sense of them. We have heard them ask: "What is this?" "How does it work?" "Can I play?" If these objects and experiences continue to interest children, they eventually put them to use, making them part of their world.

What young children do to learn about their world can provide guideposts for structuring learning experiences in school. Children's sense of wonder and excitement makes them prime candidates for approaching learning as inquiry—that is, for formulating questions, interacting with a phenomenon under study, exploring what meanings it holds for them and others, and modifying their existing theories about how the world works and is organized. In short, for figuring out stuff.

Learning as inquiry—an inquiry-based curriculum—is good for all students, including English learners. Regardless of language ability, all children are curious about their world and how it works. They all have compelling questions that arise from direct experience. And, regardless of language spoken, they have background knowledge, opinions, and other intellectual resources they can bring to what is being studied. English learners may have to find creative ways to communicate their understandings. Maybe they demonstrate; maybe they draw; maybe they find a translator. But they can and should be productive contributors to the knowledge the class is constructing. They are not the ones who decide whether there's room for them to contribute; it is the teacher— you—who decides whether to create conditions that allow all students to actively engage in learning in the classroom.

Four Approaches to an Inquiry-Based Curriculum

Daniel Callison (1999), who writes extensively about inquiry, has described four approaches to inquiry-based instruction:

Controlled Inquiry

In this approach, the teacher identifies topics and provides the necessary resources. As the students carry out their investigations, the teacher highlights a few inquiry skills explicitly, such as raising questions, seeking information from a variety of sources, and conducting interviews.

Third-grade teacher Casey Bilger carried out a controlled inquiry with his students on the topic of immigration. He carefully chose and made available resources that dealt with people emigrating from Mexico to the U.S. and addressed issues related to social justice. The resources for this study were limited mostly to books and song lyrics. He also made the decision about what the final presentation would be: Students would create a mural to display new understandings about immigration. One of Casey's major goals was to have students learn to read and respond to text from an inquiry stance rather than a retelling stance. He therefore read aloud or conducted picture walks with several picture books and provided a set of response prompts for students to use, such as "I noticed . . . ," I wonder . . . ," I thought . . ." The prompts resulted in responses such as these: "I noticed Cesar was not allowed to speak English in school," "I wonder why the family lived in a tent," and "I thought the marchers would get in trouble with the police." Later, Casey had the children revisit their responses and sort them into categories that he had generated from the students' questions (e.g., living conditions, language use, coming together to help each other). These categories and the students' responses formed the basis for the mural's content. (Segments from this unit are featured in the Extra Clips section of the DVD.)

Guided Inquiry

In guided inquiry, all students have the same inquiry topic; all are expected to deal with the same amount of information and to make the same or similar presentations. Research skills, however, are taught in a more natural flow of question-raising and information-seeking.

The inquiry project, "Motion and Design," presented in the DVD that accompanies this book might be considered guided inquiry. All the students were exploring the concept of motion and design. All were provided the same materials and information, and all were guided through experiments in which they learned to make predictions about what would make a vehicle move certain distances within certain time frames. However, in this study, much more attention was given to the inquiry process, including how to ask good questions, how to design and redesign projects based on experimentation, and how to record observations and analyze data.

Modeled Inquiry

Modeled inquiry is a more independent process. Here, the student is an apprentice in the inquiry process but has freedom to choose questions and methods. Modeled inquiry tends to work best when teachers involved have themselves been successful in completing inquiry projects. They do research alongside the students and share in the excitement of discovery.

Alyssa, a primary-grade student, had watched the movie *Finding Nemo* (Walters, 2003) and read the book *The Rainbow Fish* (Pfister, 1992). These experiences made Alyssa wonder how fish breathe, how they sleep, why they have fins, and if they really have sparkly scales. To support Alyssa's wonderings, the teacher, Mrs. Anderson, worked alongside Alyssa to find answers to her questions. The teacher located good Web sites to help her get started. She also invited Alyssa on a virtual trip to the Monterey Bay Aquarium. Mrs. Anderson then worked with Alyssa and a friend to prepare a puppet show focusing on the questions Alyssa had about fish. (Adapted from Cases: Fish Are Friends! http://virtualinquiry.com/cases/elementary15.htm.)

Free Inquiry

Free inquiry requires the highest level of independent engagement. The student is completely in charge of the entire process, from raising questions to completing a final project, and justifying the mode of presentation. In this form of inquiry, students need prior experience and practice in the process.

In Karen Smith's fifth- and sixth-grade classroom, expert projects were examples of free inquiry. On any given day, you could find students exploring topics in which they wished to gain expertise, such as how different cultures celebrate the rite of passage into puberty, how to build a generator, how Roman and Egyptian mythology are alike and different, and so on. These students had previous experience with controlled and guided inquiry. They knew how to formulate good questions and how to use their inquiry questions to determine appropriate methods and resources. They had practice in interviewing, conducting experiments, and recording and analyzing data, and they were accustomed to presenting their findings using different forms of communication. Two girls exploring rites of passage into puberty carried out a comparative study between ceremonies for Latino and Navajo girls. They wanted to know why each culture valued this rite of passage, so they used books and interviews to find out. To learn more about the rituals involved in the event, they located videos that helped them see, hear, and experience them. They were curious about how young girls today felt about this experience, so they set up interviews with girls who had recently taken part in these rites of passage. They organized their findings using T-charts and Venn diagrams to answer their questions and to compare one rite of passage to the other. To share their findings, they wrote a script about each culture's rite of passage and recruited several classmates to perform the scripts.

Conditions That Support an Inquiry-Based Curriculum

Inquiry environments must be physically, socially, and academically supportive. If students don't feel accepted by others and if they don't feel their ideas are valued, they will not engage in learning experiences, no matter how interesting or challenging they may be.

The physical setup should be arranged to accommodate project work, so it looks more like a workshop than a traditional classroom setting. Most likely, tables or desks pushed together to form tables fill much of the space. At any given time, you might see some students working on an experiment, some reading books or watching a DVD related to their inquiry topic, and others working in small groups with the teacher as she helps them make sense of what they are learning. All necessary materials for conducting an inquiry are available to students, and teachers very deliberately show students where these materials are located, how to retrieve them, and how to use them and return them, so that eventually these actions are carried out independent of the teacher. While teaching these procedures takes time, it is time well spent. Students become responsible users and consumers of resources, and teachers are freed to do the intellectual work they are hired to do.

Besides creating physical spaces for students to work independently and productively, inquiry-based classrooms require social spaces where students feel free to try out new ideas with other students. These spaces are where students put ideas out for the first time, and they need to know they can do this safely. These are spaces where there is no ridicule, no reprimand, and also no "right answers." Instead, these spaces are where ideas are answered with possibilities, questions, and ponderings. This is where ideas are listened to for content, and not for grammatical structure. And this is where students learn there are many ways to know and understand the world, and that they are responsible for entertaining multiple possibilities before presenting their new understandings to others.

The academic environment, too, must be supportive—promoting serious academic growth. While students know their ideas are accepted without ridicule, they also know and expect to be challenged in ways that are uplifting, exciting, and demanding. They are asked to think deeply about what they are learning, to seek out evidence to back up their claims, learning as they go that this is what people do when they are passionate about making sense of their world. The greatest benefit of an inquiry-based curriculum is that all students learn how to learn, and they develop habits of mind that stay with them for years to come.

Knowledge of Inquiry Processes and Elements

Students who subscribe to inquiry have a desire to understand something deeply. They are willing to engage in sustained, rigorous work. Because inquiry is often messy, recursive, and hard to pin down, and because it varies according to the content being investigated, it requires teachers' skill in nurturing habits of mind that support it.

A focus on the following four elements of inquiry can help turn an ordinary unit of study into an inspiring experience in learning that enlists students' natural curiosity and moves them toward greater understanding.

- Building Background Knowledge
- Foregrounding Student Questions
- Focusing and Conducting an Actual Study
- Presenting New Learning

Ernestina Aragón and Rebecca Osorio infused each of these elements into a pre-packaged science unit they implemented in their fifth-grade classrooms with English learners and English speakers working side by side. These two teachers have been working together for eight years. Their classrooms are adjacent to each other with a door between them that allows a constant back-and-forth flow of students, materials, and ideas. Ernestina and Rebecca often planned content units together, debriefed with one another about what did and didn't work, and revised their plans accordingly. While they had freedom in some areas of the curriculum, the science curriculum was mandated.

What Ernestina and Rebecca did was turn the mandated unit, already somewhat inquiry-based, toward more intensive inquiry. The result was a guided inquiry based on Callison's four approaches to inquiry described above. The inquiry topic was common across both classes, and all students were expected to deal with the same amount of information and to make the same or similar presentations. Research skills were taught in a natural flow of question raising and information seeking.

In this particular study, students explored physics concepts related to motion, such as force, friction, stored energy, and air resistance, and then applied these to designing vehicles. After several days of building background by messing around and experimenting with these concepts, the mandated science unit "challenged" students to design a vehicle to meet specific requirements. Each fifth-grade class was divided into seven groups of students, and each group was given a different design challenge. For example, one group had to create a pizza delivery vehicle carrying a load of pizzas (wooden blocks) that would move forward at least three meters in four seconds or less, unload the pizzas, and go back to the starting line in seven seconds or less. Each group made a final presentation to classmates and to a third-grade class, showing how their vehicle met the design challenge and explaining what they did to make it happen.

Even though the major focus of this packaged unit was science, and even though it offered materials to carry out a guided inquiry, Ernestina and Rebecca revised it to increase the level of inquiry. They added new kinds of language and literacy experiences for students to use while investigating their topics. They paid attention to grouping by deliberating putting the most patient English speakers with the least proficient English learners, thus promoting language development for all students. And they infused this packaged science unit with the four elements of inquiry we identified earlier.

In the rest of this chapter, we will pull the curtain back and show you the magic—except it isn't really magic. It is what you, too, can do with any content. We begin as Ernestina and Rebecca did—with building students' background knowledge.

NOTE: The Web site www.ncsu.edu/kenanfellows/2004/cswink/home.html contains information similar to the prepackaged material lessons for designing, building, and testing a powered vehicle that Rebecca and Ernestina used as a basis for their inquiry unit.

Building Background Knowledge

Students learn more effectively and with more enthusiasm when what they are learning is linked to what they already know. This is especially important when working with children from different linguistic and cultural backgrounds because it allows each student to filter and make sense of what they are learning through their own culture and experiences.

Finding Relevant Topics

For inquiry units to be successful, they must focus on topics relevant to students' lives. Topics become relevant as students take them up as interesting and take them on as something to work with. Even if the topic is mandated, as was the case with the unit on motion and design, teachers have to find ways to make it relevant. Ernestina's and Rebecca's emphasis on experiments is what captured students' interest and made the physics concepts relevant.

When students bring up topics themselves, the relevance is clear. An example here occurred during writing workshop. A small group of Ernestina's students noticed authors using code switching, moving from one language to another (English to Spanish) in their writing, so the students decided to try out code switching in their own writing. Ernestina encouraged this group of students and guided them through an inquiry in which they explored authors' uses of code switching, analyzing how authors used it and where they used it, and pondering possibilities for why they chose to use it (Ray, 1999). The most exciting topics of inquiry, and often the most successful, are ones students generate for themselves. When they have named a piece of the world they want to explore, and they have the skills, time, and materials to do it, we can be sure they will learn and grow from the experience.

But compelling inquiry studies can also grow out of a teacher's interest, one she is passionate about and wants to share with her class. As noted earlier, Arizona third-grade teacher Casey Bilger was passionate about immigration issues and ways immigration laws have impacted the lives of people he cared about, including the lives of some of his students. Together, Casey and his students explored these issues with enthusiasm, as shown in the Extra Clips.

Investing in the Topic

Having a topic that matters is only the beginning. Kids need to be invested in the topic. Because we know this, many of us often begin building students' background knowledge about a topic by having them share what they know and what they want to know using a graphic organizer such as a web or a K-W-L chart (*K*now, *W*ant to Know, *L*earned) (Ogle, 1986). There's no doubt this experience helps to organize what kids know about a topic; however, we aren't convinced that K-W-L questions provide the best starting point for inquiry. It has been our experience that students generate better questions and are better prepared to examine a topic critically if they know something about it before they formulate questions (Allen, 2000). It's pretty common for students to offer very little when they are asked—cold—what they know about a topic. And too often, when they are asked what they want to know, the answer is a shrug—"I don't know."

Allen believes students respond like this because they need more background knowledge *before* they know enough to want to know more. To address this issue, she adapted Ogle's K-W-L chart into the graphic organizers *Writing to Learn* and *B-K-W-L-Q* (*B*uild *B*ackground, What Do I *K*now?, What Do I *W*ant to Know?, What Did I *L*earn?, What New *Q*uestions Do I Have?). Figures 1.1 and 1.2 show these organizers.

Students use these charts before a study "officially" begins. They use them to record information and questions that emerge during four or five experiences related to their topic. After participating in these experiences, students have more information and also more ideas about what they want to know. In other words, they are ready to carry out an informed investigation of their topic. These two graphic organizers are flexible and can be used across content areas and with any number of reading, listening, viewing, and tactile experiences, as long as each experience builds on previous learning and leads students to develop their own questions.

In the unit on motion and design, Rebecca and Ernestina relied mostly on tactile experiences to help students build background and generate questions about what they knew and what they wanted to know about motion and design. They began by presenting mini-lessons on concepts of motion and design. After each mini-lesson, small groups of students worked together to make sense of the concept by constructing vehicles from the packaged parts. They used a range of materials to manipulate variables—sometimes creating different forms of energy, sometimes determining the effect of weight on a vehicle, and sometimes trying out ways friction affects a vehicle's motion. In each case, students documented their observations, compared information,

Writing to Learn

Source:	Source:	Source:
Facts:	Facts:	Facts:
Response:	Response:	Response:

	Connections:
	  I wonder:
	
	  I want to know:
		Connections:
		  Now that I know _____
		  I'm interested in knowing _____
		  _____
		  _____
		  _____
		  _____

Figure 1.1: **Writing to Learn** (From *Yellow Brick Roads: Shared and Guided Paths to Independent Reading 4–12* by Janet Allen, copyright © 2000, reprinted with permission of Stenhouse Publishers.)

B-K-W-L-Q

Build Background	What Do I Know?	What Do I Want to Know?	What Did I Learn?	What New Questions Do I Have?

Figure 1.2: **B-K-W-L-Q** (From *Yellow Brick Roads: Shared and Guided Paths to Independent Reading 4–12* by Janet Allen, copyright © 2000, reprinted with permission of Stenhouse Publishers.)

and considered the relevance of what they were learning to the bigger idea of motion and design. On *Writing to Learn* charts, students categorized the information they had gleaned from the experiences. Figure 1.3 shows the Writing to Learn chart Ernestina and Rebecca adapted that focused on facts, wonderings, and students' responses to two experiments and the viewing of a video.

The chart on page 28 shows one student's response to three experiences. Students used the same kind of chart to respond to other experiments, readings, and DVDs related to their topics. The important point is that by the time students were given a design challenge, where they were required to design a vehicle according to a set of specifications, they had background to draw on. When they were asked about what they knew, they had something to say. When asked what they wanted to know, their list went on and on, and, perhaps most important, they had questions to consider as they generated predictions about what vehicle design would best meet a specific challenge. These questions provided a more substantive basis for inquiry than what could have been elicited at the beginning of a study by filling in the "K" (What Do I Know?) column of a K-W-L chart

Foregrounding Student Questions

The mandated commercial science program did not foreground students' questions, but Rebecca and Ernestina did—and they did it by having students list what they were wondering about throughout the study. For example, they wanted students to see the value of the questions they had generated during the background-building phase of the study. So when the students began to design the vehicle to meet the "official challenge," the teachers took the "wondering" statements and questions students had written on the Writing to Learn charts and put them into larger categories (see Figure 1.4).

Once each group received its design challenge, the students read through this list of questions and highlighted those that fit their particular challenge and used them as one resource to create their design plan. For example, the students who had to design a vehicle that could go a long distance in a short time highlighted the following questions as they began their design:

- Will a car go faster if we use three wheels in the back instead of two?
- What kind of surface will make my vehicle go really fast?
- Will the vehicle go faster if we change the angle of the rod?

Writing to Learn

Source: **Experiment— Creating a Vehicle**	Source: **Experiment Using Falling Weight System**	Source: **Viewing Video— *Bill Nye the Science Guy on Friction***
Facts: Vehicles have wheels. The less weight I put on the car, the faster it went. The more weight I put on the car, the slower it went. A vehicle is safer with a bumper than without one. A design affects the vehicle's movement.	**Facts:** The more washers we put in the cup, the faster the car went. Force can move a lot of things. Weight creates force and speed.	**Facts:** The harder things rub together, the more friction they make. Athletes wear shoes with cleats to make friction. Friction affects the movement and speed of a vehicle.
Wonderings: I wonder which vehicle could win a race. I wonder if I could stop my vehicle with a parachute.	**Wonderings:** I wonder how far the vehicle would go if the bookend wasn't here to stop it. I wonder what we will have to do to make enough force for the vehicle to go up a ramp.	**Wonderings:** I wonder what kind of surface (friction) we can use to make our vehicle go faster.
Responses: I think the vehicle should have hydraulics. I would like to make an electric car. The first time I saw what we had to do, I thought, "I can't do it."	**Responses:** I want to try this with a runway that is longer than the table we used today. Our string was too long and we didn't get to see what happens when the cup doesn't touch the floor.	**Responses:** I want to try my vehicle on the sidewalk and not on the carpet to see if it goes faster.

Figure 1.3: **Writing to Learn** (From *Yellow Brick Roads: Shared and Guided Paths to Independent Reading 4–12* by Janet Allen, copyright © 2000, reprinted with permission of Stenhouse Publishers.)

Side-by-Side Learning

Design Plan: Energy Sources

- What would happen if we used both rubber-band and falling-weight energy?
    - I wonder how many washers we need to make a car go fast.
    - How do you slow down a vehicle when it is going fast?
    - Will a car go faster if we use three wheels in the back instead of two?
    - What kind of surface will make my vehicle go really fast?
    - Will the vehicle go faster if we change the angle of the rod?

Figure 1.4: Sample of categories and questions from *Writing to Learn* charts

These "wonderings" provided a starting point for designing their vehicle. More important, they validated students' thinking and made it part of the official curriculum.

Rebecca and Ernestina also used students' questions to help students learn to pose conceptually rich questions rather than merely questions of fact. To begin this process, they provided the criteria listed in Figure 1.5 for posing good questions.

Students used these criteria to hone their questioning skills. To do this, Ernestina and Rebecca asked each student to copy two of the inquiry questions they had already written on their *Writing to Learn* chart onto two separate sticky notes. In the meantime, the teachers hung a large chart on the whiteboard in front of the class with the following column headings: Yes/No Questions; Vague Questions; Unanswerable Questions; Not Doable Questions given time and materials available; and Doable, Answerable Questions with Specific Information (see Figure 1.6).

The teachers then guided students through an analytic process. First, they had students read their questions to see if one or both could be answered with "yes" or "no." If so, the students attached their sticky note on the "Yes/No Questions" column of the chart. Next, students silently read their remaining question(s) and determined if they fit any of the next three columns, and, if so, why. Individual students were called on to share their question, tell where it fit on the chart and why, and then post it in the appropriate column. Examples of questions students wrote that fit the categories on the chart included the following:

> ## What Makes a Good Question?
>
> A GOOD question is one that:
>
> - we don't already know the answer to
> - cannot be answered with "yes" or "no"
> - has specific rather than vague content
> - is researchable, that is, you must be able to collect evidence to answer it
> - is doable, given materials and time available

Figure 1.5: Criteria for Good Questions

Yes/No questions:	Does rubber-band energy work?
Vague questions:	How much weight do we need?
Unanswerable questions:	What forms of energy will humans use in the 22nd century?
Not doable questions:	What would happen if I used hydraulics to fuel my car?
Doable, answerable questions with information:	What will happen to the speed of our vehicle if we change the angle of the axle?

Once the questions were categorized, Ernestina and Rebecca used the questions from the first four columns and worked with the students to turn them into good inquiry questions (doable, answerable questions with information). They wanted students to understand that the intent of a question may be right, but if it isn't worded with care and specificity, it may limit the depth of understandings that emerge from their inquiry.

For example, instead of asking, "Does rubber-band energy work?" they asked, "How many times do we have to wind the rubber band to make our vehicle go three meters?"

Helping students formulate good inquiry questions is important. So are the manner and types of questions teachers ask throughout the inquiry process. Paul Houghtaling (2003) argues that questioning is one of the most profound inquiry tools available. A good question, he claims, can drive the senses to become more deeply involved in what we are experiencing; it can bring us

Categories of Questions

Yes/No Questions, Specific	Vague Questions	Unanswerable Questions	Not Doable Questions	Doable, Answerable Questions With Information

Figure 1.6: **Categories of Questions**

deeply into the moment—present to us the wondrous and mysterious things happening around and within us. He then reminds us that questions also can be hurtful. We think this is an especially important message when working with English learners. As we question students, we need to read body language and pay attention to what it reveals. If it cues discomfort, it may mean the student is shutting down from further engagement and further learning. If we notice students shutting down or not participating, the following levels of questioning strategies based on those described by Tom Baker (cited in Houghtaling, 2003) may bring them back into the process.

1. **Ask a question the students can answer.** This builds confidence in their ability to answer what is asked of them (and also shows the questioner some of what the student knows). When Rebecca asked, "Juan, do you want to use the falling-weight system or rubber-band energy today?" she was asking a question at this level.

2. **Ask a question that is on the edge of the student's awareness and knowledge, but which still requires some thought.** Ernestina's question to Maurice, "Which direction will your car move if you wind the rubber band under the axle?" was one such question. Maurice

already had experience moving the vehicle using rubber-band energy, but he had to think about the difference it made when he wound the rubber band under the axle rather than over it.

3. **Ask a question that is beyond the student's ability to answer and which opens up a new realm of what is possible.** When Rebecca posed a question about the effect weight has on the distance vehicles travel, she was asking a level 3 question.

Good questions are critical to a successful inquiry, but they are only part of the solution. Another is to help students focus and conduct their study.

Focusing and Conducting an Actual Study

Once students gain background knowledge about their topic and develop research questions that lead to meaningful investigations, they are ready to begin a focused inquiry. Rebecca and Ernestina relied on materials from a science kit to focus their students' inquiries. The students began by selecting a design challenge to solve, knowing they would be using concepts and ideas they had explored during the background-building phase of the study. Like engineers, they were expected to plan, build, test, evaluate, modify, and retest their vehicle before presenting it to an audience. Figure 1.7 shows the process plan that Rebecca and Ernestina created to guide students as they worked through their design.

These teachers took nothing for granted. They did not assume kids were familiar with conducting an inquiry on their own; they didn't assume English learners would understand the challenge simply by reading it and working with peers; and they didn't expect students to have full control of the academic language needed to articulate their understandings about their final product.

Process for Solving a Design Challenge:
- Read design challenge and create a plan to solve it.
- Design a vehicle based on plan.
- Test and evaluate design.
- Modify and Retest design.

Figure 1.7: **Plan for Designing and Building Vehicle**

So they walked students through the "official challenge" step by step, with demonstrations to the whole class and guidance to groups and individuals on an "as needed" basis. First, both Rebecca and Ernestina urged students to take it slow as they planned their designs. They reminded them to read their challenge carefully and to refer to it over and over again. They urged them to think about the best type of force and load for their challenge; to review what they had already written on charts and think about implications for their current design; to find other resources if necessary; and then to create a design for their vehicle, knowing they would have to test the design, modify it, and test it again until it met their specifications.

On the first day of the focused study, each teacher hung a large chart on the board that looked exactly like the chart they would provide each group. A design challenge similar to the ones the students would be conducting was glued to the top of the chart, and underneath it were two columns, one labeled "Questions" and the other "Ideas for Solving the Design Challenge" (see Figure 1.8).

This whole-group experience, like the small-group experiences that would follow, relied on students' knowledge of the concepts and language they had been working with during the background-building phase of the study.

Once the students had ideas for solving this design challenge, Ernestina and Rebecca provided a large-scale, more in-depth outline to guide their work (see Figure 1.9).

The section titled "How we will meet the challenge *as a group*" was added to the plan based on the teachers' observations the previous day that particular students were dominating the talk and activity in the small groups. The teachers approached this topic positively by focusing on criteria a group should use to work together successfully to meet their shared goal. They then explored the responsibilities and rights of group members. The teachers wanted to make sure all students understood they had a responsibility to contribute to the vehicle's final design, and that they each had the right to have their ideas heard and considered with respect.

Presenting New Learning

Ernestina and Rebecca created opportunities for students to share new understandings with new audiences, to see firsthand that their learning was useful beyond their own classroom. All too frequently, teachers have relied on

Design Challenge

Challenge E

You are part of a famous engineering design team. An agency has just awarded your team a contract to design a drag racing car. The dragster must move a relatively short distance as quickly as possible and then come to a stop.

Design Requirements:

- In 2 seconds or less, your vehicle must move from the starting line to the finish line.

- The distance of the race track is 2 m (6.56 ft.).

- Your vehicle must stop within 50 cm (20 in.) of the finish line.

- You may drag weights or other objects behind your vehicle to slow it down.

Cost is important. You must build the vehicle as inexpensively as possible without affecting its performance.

From National Science Resources Center (2003). *Motion and Design* (Science and Technology for Children Books). Washington, DC: National Academies Press.

QUESTIONS	IDEAS FOR SOLVING THE DESIGN CHALLENGE

Figure 1.8: **Example of Chart for Planning the Design Challenge**

Planning Our Final Design Challenge

- Ideas to meet the challenge
- Sketch of the vehicle we will build
- How we will move our vehicle
- Materials needed to build vehicle
- Materials needed to move vehicle
- Tools needed to test whether vehicle meets the challenge
- How will we meet the challenge as a group

Figure 1.9: **Final Planning Sheet**

written reports as the preferred way to share new understandings. But written reports are just one way to share knowledge and often not even a particularly good way. Instead, means of reporting should fit the topic and the audience.

Ernestina and Rebecca took their cue from the prepackaged materials and had students use a chart to make a formal presentation to an out-of-class audience. The chart displayed the challenge, the process the group went through to design their vehicle, problems they had to overcome, and solutions they devised. Students concluded their presentations by demonstrating their vehicle meeting (or not meeting) the challenge.

In creating the chart for the formal presentation, the students used writing workshop time to draft, revise, and edit their written display. This included the text of the challenge, a list of the problems and solutions that guided their inquiry, and blueprints of the initial and final designs. The students created their final charts on a word processor, and the teachers enlarged and then printed each of them onto a 28" x 36" chart. Students then used these charts to guide their oral presentation. This was useful to all students, but especially to the English learners. They all participated in the oral presentations based on their proficiency and level of comfort with English. They were given several opportunities to practice, so when the day came to present, they were familiar with their part of the presentation. Some English learners chose to read the challenge. Others presented the problems and often relied on the written text, simply reading what was there. More proficient speakers talked through the problems and solutions, improvising on the text and answering questions throughout the presentation. One student new to the classroom who understood and spoke very little English had the job of reading the headings on the chart: *Design Challenge, Problem, Solution*. She practiced saying these three terms over and over again before the actual presentation. She was as proud of her contribution as the native English speaker who spoke eloquently about force, friction, and weight and about the interpersonal dynamics that required working through the design challenge.

Assessment

Assessment is a necessary part of good teaching. As Ernestina and Rebecca continued to develop an inquiry stance in their classrooms, they generated assessment forms and techniques that captured the complexities of their students' learning. They relied heavily on portfolio assessment for chronicling students' work. In the motion and design unit, students' portfolios included *Writing to Learn* data, logs with data from experiments, responses to readings and viewings about force, blueprints of vehicle designs, planning forms, and their final write-up for presentation. Throughout this and other inquiry studies, Ernestina and Rebecca often used a form similar to Figure 1.10 to assess each student's participation in the unit.

All students can learn to be investigators and creators of knowledge—and all teachers (yes, you too) can become guides for such activity. All students can learn to tap into their curiosities, think deeply and critically about them, and take the initiative to learn more—and all teachers can help them do that. All students—and all teachers (including you)—can become confident risk-takers who understand that learning is messy and indeterminate, and requires patience, time, and lots of trial and error. Through inquiry, students can develop habits of lifelong learning—and teachers (every one of us) can teach all students side by side.

Inquiry-Based Assessment

Name _____ Date _____

PROCESS	COMMENTS
Uses appropriate methods for gathering data (e.g., writing letters, interviewing, experimenting, observing, reading, etc.)	
Formulates good questions	
Spends time reading, writing, observing, reflecting, etc.	
Asks good questions	
Explains, demonstrates, helps others	
Plans, organizes, and carries through on tasks	
Understands new ideas	

ATTITUDE	COMMENTS
Is willing to be challenged	
Is productive during work time	
Contributes willingly to group work	
Displays sensitivity and respect for others	
Learns from watching and working with others	

PRODUCT	COMMENTS
Is well developed and organized	
Is visually pleasing	
Provides detail	
Communicates Effectively what student has learned	

PRESENTATION	COMMENTS
Articulates and/or demonstrates ideas clearly	
Is well informed	
Handles questions with authority and control	
Gives good examples	

Figure 1.10: **Inquiry Assessment Form** (adapted from Reimer, Stephens, & Smith, 1993)

CHAPTER 2

Support for Second Language Learning Through Inquiry-Based Curriculum

Meaningful learning takes place in an environment that encourages thoughtfulness. . . . All kids, and especially English language learners, will learn and flourish in an environment that focuses on thinking and understanding.

Anne Goudvis,
foreword to *Ladybugs, Tornadoes, and Swirling Galaxies: English Language Learners Discover Their World Through Inquiry*

We've been making what might seem to be a startling claim: Inquiry elements can help you teach all students side by side. But inquiry elements alone are not enough. To help the English learners in your classroom, you also need to follow two principles: 1) Support and 2) Stretch. This chapter is about those principles and about how to bring them to life.

Together, SUPPORT and STRETCH principles provide a foundation for the kinds of strategies and practices you can use in any content area with an inquiry-based curriculum. In the sections that follow, we will give examples of strategies and practices that reflect both SUPPORT and STRETCH principles. For each strategy and practice, it will be helpful if you consider the following questions:

- Do I understand how the strategy or practice relates to the SUPPORT principle, the STRETCH principle, or both?
- How does the strategy or practice specifically support language learning while students are engaged in inquiry?

- How often and when should I use the strategy or practice?
- What other strategies and practices do I use to promote SUPPORT and STRETCH principles?

The SUPPORT Principle

For all students to participate regardless of their language proficiency, they'll need support. Sometimes, support refers to extra cues you can give English learners so they can make better sense of what's going on. Sometimes, support is a matter of putting just the right English learners and English speakers into a small group and then giving the group lots of time to talk with one another about academic work. Sometimes, support comes from the kinds of reading and writing that students do as part of their work on academic content. When you add all these up, the result is support for English learners so they can participate and learn along with everyone else.

SUPPORT During Inquiry Learning Experiences

As we said in Chapter 1, inquiry-based content units are much more fruitful if students increase their background knowledge about a topic before they even begin investigating it. When students become somewhat familiar with major concepts related to a topic, they can formulate better questions and also relate what they're finding out to the larger topic. The nine strategies and practices we present below, all following from the SUPPORT principle, can help you provide—guess what!—support! Simultaneously, these strategies and practices that provide support for English learners as they build background knowledge of the topic under study can also enable students to STRETCH the ways they use oral and written language.

Say It With Support

One of the best ways to support English learners is to use gestures and facial expressions. We all use our hands and facial expressions to talk about ideas and actions. In a classroom setting, bodily and facial gestures—including pointing to words and objects—are indispensable for soliciting ideas, recalling highlights, and going over procedures. Teachers who understand the SUPPORT principle know that gestures, such as pointing to key written words or pictures in a book, waving arms to show movement, holding up fingers while discussing quantities, and marking space with hand movements, help English learners understand language they might not have gotten otherwise. For instance, imagine you were talking with a group of English learners about the force of wind coming at you in a car, as Ernestina was doing with a small group. Using gestures to show the consequence of that force supports meaning; it helps English learners see as well as hear what is going on.

There are many times during a school day when you can combine facial expressions with physical gesticulations to indicate surprise, joy, sadness, astonishment, and wonderment. Although some of the facial expressions you use to convey emotions may not be entirely cross-cultural, English learners who are new to U.S. schools soon learn, from repetition in other contexts, to interpret the meanings of these facial expressions and gesticulations in ways you have intended. Finally, facial expressions coupled with body gestures send the message to students that you are listening to them, that you are interested in what they have to contribute, and that you appreciate their efforts to express their knowledge. This helps build classroom solidarity and community, which in turn helps all students feel safe. And feeling safe is crucial for language learning.

Convey It With Multimedia

In addition to gestures, visual aids provide scaffolds for English learners. "A picture is worth a thousand words" may be a cliché but it is relevant here. Similar to gestures, visual aids, such as PowerPoint presentations, DVDs, YouTube clips, photographs, artwork, maps, and graphic organizers, are especially important for building background. In going beyond spoken and written text, they help students see in a flash what might otherwise have remained fuzzy.

Films, film clips, and photographs can help students experience visually the various ways that knowledge can be organized. For example, a sequence can be made visible with a time line. A map can show relative distance between places in Mexico and places in the U.S. A web can serve as a springboard to categorize ideas that at first glance seem disparate. Showing how to fill out and use a Venn diagram can help students visually detect where ideas are similar or different. In a study of immigration, third-grade teacher Casey Bilger was helping students build background on the lives of immigrants (available in the Extra Clips section of the DVD). He used a projector to show larger images of various books depicting immigrants' lives so that students could see what was being discussed and use the vocabulary related to what was shown on the enlarged pages. Then the students worked together to cluster ideas and compare these with what they knew from stories they had heard in their own families. These experiences helped students learn about and incorporate new facts as well as new language about reasons for immigration and difficulties experienced by immigrants.

Put It on a Chart

Most presentations outside of school use some form of a chart to highlight key points. Throughout the inquiry unit shown on the DVD, the teachers used charts with the whole class to recap what students learned and to help teach what counts as a good question. The teachers also asked students to use charts individually and in small groups to coauthor their observations, questions, and wonderings. Making and using charts (these can include drawings, pictures, and writing) offers SUPPORT to all students, but especially to English learners. Charts help students visually organize important ideas. They show students how words and phrases used in speech look when they are written. And because they lend themselves to coproduction by members of a small group, their creation offers English learners new ways to participate. For instance, in creating a chart for a PowerPoint presentation, English learners can help choose the slide design and layout, along with the fonts, font size, and colors—and, importantly, take part in discussing the decision. If a paper chart is being constructed, English learners working alongside teammates can make drawings, copy facts, and contribute to the wording of each main section. Such collaborations are likely to involve English learners in reading and writing summary information, writing down steps and procedures, and, of course, highlighting questions that were answered and questions that remain—all ways of using language to support English learners and English learning.

Up to this point, we have recommended obvious kinds of support—gestures and a variety of visual aids. There are other less obvious strategies that also support English learners because they make it easier for them to more actively participate and use the language they are just beginning to learn.

Give Students Time to Think and Respond

English learners often need extra time to think about how to say what they want to say in response to open-ended questions. In classrooms where English learners and English speakers learn side by side, extra wait time evens the playing field. Suppose you are working at the whiteboard getting ready to write down students' questions about what they have read. You can pick the students with their hands up first, or, as Rebecca Osorio did on the DVD when she asked a question and many hands sprang up, you can wait and ask everyone to think a bit longer about the answer, allowing more students to participate. Not only does extra wait time provide additional time for English learners to think about how they want to respond, it also sets the pace of interaction and encourages all students to think beyond their initial reactions.

Encourage Students to Use Their Primary Language

Inquiry work should provide students with many occasions for working with others in small groups or pairs. During those times, English learners who speak the same primary language can exchange ideas, ask for clarification, and discuss word meanings in that language—and they'll do that openly and confidently if you encourage it. Using the primary language enables English learners, especially students who are brand-new to English, to stay involved in discussions. The primary language supports learning because it lets students share information and feel safer and less vulnerable. Of equal importance, it also conveys to students that their primary language is a valuable medium for learning. When students use their primary language to make sense of discussions, they are more likely to continue their participation, and when called upon they can contribute on the basis of what they have understood and learned. Isn't this what we all want for our students?

Take Dictation

Writing down what is said—especially when what is said is part of a list of responses to a question or even the question itself—provides written support for learning in a new language. English learners typically do not understand all of what is said by the teacher and classmates. And, indeed, all literacy learners need to see how spoken language looks in written form. Seeing written forms of words and phrases helps students flesh out the ideas being discussed and also the image (in sound and sight) of individual words. For example, if you were to ask a group of English learners and English speakers sitting side by side an open-ended question such as "What's going to happen when we turn the wheels this way rather than that way?" an English learner may hear *whats gonna happ'n unwe turn wheels this way ratherun that way.* When you write down what you say so that all students can see what you have said, you allow students to fill in the blanks they may have missed orally and to see word boundaries.

Likewise, when you write down what students say exactly as they say it, you affirm the student's ability to communicate and participate in the conversation. If an English learner responds to the above question with "Is going backward this way, and front this way," you need to find *a phrase* (not necessarily every word the student said) that you can write exactly as the student said it—e.g., "going backward this way." If the student's contribution is a global goof—every phrase is so full of errors it is nearly incomprehensible (e.g., "the wheels is go here forward back for there")—then try to lift the level of the contribution by translating it into a short phrase that might represent at least some of the meaning the student intended. (You can often figure that out from the context and the student's body language.) In this example, you might write "goes back." In any case, it's important to give some credit to the student by putting her contribution on the chart. This enables the student to see in written form some of what she herself has said. It gives you— the teacher—a chance to show the student that she has made a genuine contribution. And it also lets you extend and build on that contribution. Moreover, you show not only the student but also everyone else that you value the contribution. Displaying such valuing in front of the class—i.e., in public— creates a climate that encourages all students to participate and to recognize the value of others' contributions.

Incorporate Demonstrations

One of the ways that English learners can share what they know is by using non-verbal demonstrations to fill in gaps in their new language. When students don't know particular vocabulary or ways of phrasing an idea, the teacher can either discourage or encourage them to improvise—e.g., to fill in with gestures, nearby objects, dramatization, and so on. If you insist on language only (no nonverbal fill-ins), you decrease students' participation—and participation is necessary for learning. But when you encourage such nonverbal augmentation, you allow the rest of the class to benefit from a classmate's ideas. And for the sake of language growth, you set up an all-important real context for *negotiating meaning*.

When a language learner can't quite say it and others don't quite get it, they have to *negotiate about meaning*. Such negotiation promotes learning the new language because it provides chances to hear language that clarifies, rebuts, or confirms the meanings being negotiated. Oftentimes, what the teacher or a classmate says to clarify or confirm contains the words and expressions the learner intended to use. Back-and-forth negotiations of meaning let the learner turn around and use those words and expressions right then, in context, and for real purposes of communication. Good language learners don't back away from participating just because they don't know how to say something. Instead, they negotiate meaning by filling in the gaps with gestures, objects, dramatizing, and other demonstrations. And they "argue" about interpretations ("No, that's not what I meant. Let me show you again.").

How do children become such good language learners? They learn it from you—from adults (and peers, too) who do more than talk; from adults and peers who point, gesture, show—in a word, from others who *demonstrate*. In exemplary classrooms we have observed, teachers are consistently demonstrating key ideas while they are talking with the whole class. When they walk around from small group to small group, they encourage students to demonstrate what they know, what they're thinking about, what they're wondering. And they build on the ideas being demonstrated (not only those being presented in words) so that those important back-and-forth negotiations can take place.

Ensure All Students Have Access to Participation

We have already mentioned the benefits of *wait time* for English learners. There are also other ways you can ensure that students have access to participation. When you are asking questions or asking for students' contributions in a whole-class setting, you can use the *Popsicle stick strategy*, as Casey Bilger did (you can see this in the Extra Clips section of the DVD). For this strategy,

Casey wrote each student's name on a Popsicle stick, dropped the sticks into a can, and pulled out a name after he posed a question or asked for a comment. Another strategy is to use a small ball or a beanie bag. You ask a question and then throw out the ball or beanie bag to a student. That student must respond. For the next question, the student passes the ball or beanie bag to another student, and so on.

In small-group work, you can distribute turns for talk more or less equally by using *talking chips*—some small token, such as a plastic poker chip. At the beginning of each small-group experience, you provide each student with a talking chip. Every time a students wishes to talk, he or she must place the chip in a central place, usually the center of the table or the working space on the floor. No one in the group can talk again until everyone has placed a chip into the pile, at which time the students retrieve their individual chip and the process begins anew.

Another strategy for encouraging all students to interact and to listen as others in the group speak is called *paraphrase passport*. In this strategy, access to talking stems from correctly paraphrasing the student who has just spoken. After a student in the group has contributed an idea, the new person to speak has to rephrase the idea before contributing a new idea. This strategy enables English learners to hear different ways of saying the same thing, and it encourages students to appropriate others' ways of saying things.

When students are seated on the floor or side by side at tables, you can use the *think-pair-share* strategy. You can see this in Ernestina's and Rebecca's rooms on the DVD. *Think-pair-share* is a three-step process that begins with a relatively open-ended question to all. You allow students a minute or so to contemplate how they would answer. In step two, pairs of students talk to one another about how they would answer. In the final step, students share their partner's answers with another pair. You can also have one member of the pair (or a two-pair foursome) share with the entire class some of the ideas that were generated.

Group Students With Mixed Abilities

There are several aspects to consider when you place students of mixed abilities into small groups. By mixed abilities, we don't mean just English-language proficiency. In any classroom, students have multiple abilities: Some can draw well; some can read and write well; some are bilingual and biliterate;

some can scaffold the learning of others; some can paraphrase ideas really well; some are good at following written directions; some are risk takers, and some are comfortable interacting with students who are beginning English learners. Knowing about the multiple abilities of all your students will aid you in making decisions about how to constitute groups that will be working together for longer time periods. One of the goals of strategically forming small groups is to form them in ways that provide support to English learners.

For some side-by-side interactions, it may not matter who is a good artist or who writes well. For example, when Ernestina and Rebecca are interacting with the whole class, they often ask students to pair up for a quick discussion and then share with the whole class what they discussed. Here the goal is to have students think first and then talk to one another, posing and answering questions, clarifying ideas, and so on before sharing with a larger group or even the entire class. As was mentioned above, this strategy provides English learners with time to think as well as a safe context for hearing and using language pertaining to the topic at hand. The key to success for this kind of quick pairing is to make sure that English learners who are new to English are paired with English speakers, other English learners with higher English proficiency, or students who speak their same primary language.

For groups that will be together over several weeks, it is important to take into account the social, academic, and language abilities that students bring to particular groups. In classrooms where English learners work side by side with English speakers over long periods of time, it makes a great deal of sense to strategically place English learners with classmates who are highly English proficient or with English speakers who work well with English learners. In either case, you might also think about forming groups where students share a common primary language or have varying English language proficiency. It is also important to group students who are good helpers, who have some of the abilities that will be required throughout the lesson, and who are likely to share equally in the group discussions. Many teachers assign roles to each member of a small group so that everyone in the group contributes. A particularly important role to consider is "participation monitor"—the person responsible for carrying out tasks and ensuring that everyone shares in the discussion.

The STRETCH Principle

The STRETCH principle is about a kind of teaching that *compels* English learners to understand and sometimes produce oral and written language that is *stretched slightly beyond* their present proficiency with English. Kids stretch their proficiency with English when they use it to exchange and question information, express wonder and doubt, make guesses and declarations, share feelings, and appreciate surprises. One of your tasks, therefore, is to plan in-class experiences that demand these kinds of language use. It is these experiences that will stretch students' English language abilities.

STRETCH Language to Get More Language

Supporting English learners through inquiry-based instruction augmented with the above strategies helps them use English more comfortably and, thus, more often. But you'll also want to STRETCH students' abilities to discuss and write out their thoughts in English. Inquiry-based learning assumes that students are curious and learn best when they pose and answer questions based on explorations, discussions, and focused investigation. In this section, we present four main strategies and practices that help expand the language abilities of English learners.

Write, Write, Write

Frequent informal writing helps English learners stretch their language. Quick jottings let students try out language that reinforces ideas and lets them do so with few consequences. Sometimes these quick writings are then used as raw material for a more public text to be written by a small group. Such informal writing is less risky for newcomers to English as well as for English speakers who are reluctant to write. In several of the outstanding classes we observed, students used sticky notes to jot down facts, responses to artwork, and ideas about particular passages they had read. In other classes, students wrote down their observations, sometimes in a small slot on a chart (see Figure 2.1).

In other classes, students drew their ideas first and then wrote about what they drew. When English learners write and draw, they try out new vocabulary; they think about how words are spelled; and they put into written form what

What modifications or changes need to be made in order for you to meet the challenge?

We Pot more Big washers
awD 4 litol washers
awD we ToK of The gry
coNNecTorS so The Tiyers
caN muv FasTer.

RETEST YOUR VEHICLE

What happened the 2nd time? Record your results here. What did you observe? Did you meet your design challenge? Explain.

Yes our car map The
shaleNo ageN.

Draw and color a detailed picture of your challenge.

Figure 2.1: **Student who is new to English records his observation**

they can say orally or draw visually. Notice in the writing samples how students expressed their understanding of concepts. The students used their existing knowledge about language to produce more language. When English learners draw and write down their thoughts, and others read these texts, they get multiple chances to clarify, multiple opportunities to ask for and get confirmation for what they're trying to say, and lots of practice in negotiating meaning. All these are crucial for further language learning.

Encourage Collaborative Writing

English learners learn from others how to use English according to convention. When English learners work side by side with students who have a range of writing abilities, there is a good chance that the students will help one another with their written work, especially as they get ready to write for an outside audience. When students write together, it is common to hear them discussing spelling and word choice in a safe and nonthreatening context (as you can hear on the DVD if you listen carefully).

English learners who are new to English and other students who are inexperienced writers (English-proficient or not) often find writing a challenge. In addition, they may not realize they can approach other students for help with writing. Collaborative writing reduces the difficulty because it provides on-the-spot scaffolding from fellow classmates. For example, suppose you prepared sentence starters, like the ones below, for use in small collaborative writing groups. English learners could write out the sentence starters and then get support from others to complete them. We have seen such support provided through direct modeling by other students, from group members' attention to charts they made before, and from discussions about the topic.

I now know that . . . and so I think we should . . .

What would happen if . . . ?

I didn't know that . . .

I still don't know if . . .

Brainstorming provides another opportunity for collaborative writing. Frequent brainstorming by a small group, along with writing down the brainstormed ideas, supports English learners in several ways. The goal of brainstorming is to generate—and say to others—many ideas, even ideas that aren't such good ones, to spark something that might not have otherwise been thought about. In inquiry projects, students might brainstorm subtopics to investigate, new words they've heard in discussions, "puzzlements," ways to proceed in investigating their question, places to look for information, titles for their final presentation, and so on. Students brainstorm through talk and, when talk fails them, with drawings, objects, and anything else they can use.

Brainstorming is helpful to English learners because it gives them yet another context to understand that it is ideas that count, not necessarily how you say or write them. That is, brainstorming offers support. But eventually, how ideas are said and written do count—and that's where the stretching comes in. Ideas that are brainstormed by a small group need to be written down. During the writing down, students are apt to help one another with spelling, punctuation, and writing conventions, as well as with sharpening ideas. This language work, done by learners and peers together, stretches English learners' language—and sometimes the language of more proficient English speakers, too.

Vary Questions to Students

In most classrooms, teachers pose questions that guide instruction. The bulk of these questions ask for information the teacher already knows. The main purpose of known-information questions is to check for understanding. Based on students' responses, the teacher has a good idea about where the students are with respect to what they have been studying. Many known-information questions call for a yes/no response or some other one-word response. Teachers can use easier known-information questions to build confidence in students. It feels good when a student, especially one who is new to English, can answer a question in front of peers, even if it is a simple "yes" or "no."

However, there is a downside to relying heavily on known-information questions, especially for English learners in an inquiry-based curriculum. For one thing, these kinds of questions do not push English learners to expand their thinking and to stretch their use of English, unless the questions are followed by more open-ended questions. Beyond checking for understanding, your goal should be to move the conversation forward in ways that prod students to apply their understandings, insights, and newly informed opinions to other situations. Known-information questions don't accomplish this goal. A second reason that you should avoid overusing known-information questions is that they are not good models for the kinds of questions you want students to generate for inquiry. Instead, you want to ask questions that promote reflection and deeper thinking, and that build on students' contributions by extending or reshaping them into broader issues.

Following are examples of the kinds of questions that you might ask students based on their discussions and the sources of information you would like them to extend.

Questions for open-ended "noticings":

- What other things do you notice about the family in this picture?
- What else do you notice about the items on this list?
- What other things do you notice about the way this vehicle moves?

Questions about resemblances:

- In what ways does this family remind you of your own family?
- What are the ways the items on this list resemble the items on this other list?
- How does the motion of this vehicle resemble anything else you can think of?

Questions about procedures:

- How did you make your vehicle move exactly three centimeters?
- How did you create the PowerPoint presentation you're going to show in the final presentation?

Questions requiring going beyond the material:

- Under what circumstances might the color of the vehicle affect the speed of the vehicle?
- What would your audience learn if you were to use a drama for the final presentation instead of a PowerPoint presentation?
- What will the family in this picture be doing in 20 years?

Questions requiring imagined actions for social justice:

- How can kids help feed homeless people?
- What needs to be done to improve this family's future?
- What can you do to make it safer to ride bicycles in your neighborhood?

These questions ask students to describe, compare, explain, analyze, predict, and imagine, using phrasing and vocabulary that draws on and extends what they've been discussing. If you broaden and link students' talk to bigger issues and use support strategies, it is likely that these open-ended questions will nudge English learners to try out and, consequently, to stretch their developing language.

However, if you find that a student who is still learning English can't answer these more open-ended questions with extended language, do not despair. You can always work to unpack the question and rephrase it so it can be answered with a short answer or turn it into an either/or question. For example, instead of asking what else an audience might learn from drama rather than from a "lecture," you might rephrase the question in a yes/no format: "Can you dramatize how people feel when they are forced to leave their homes and go to a strange land?" Or, in an either/or format: "Does language play a big part in difficulties faced by immigrants, or does language seem not to be very important?" Once the student provides a response, you can restate the student's comment using more general language and acknowledge the student's contribution. This also might be a time when you "translate" answers given in everyday form into more academic phrasing. So if the student says, "Immigrants have trouble with language," you can add to the conversation and the academic vocabulary by saying, "Yes, many people have trouble learning a new language, and policies about language add to the difficulties."

In some of the classes we have visited, teachers help students stretch their language by providing them with certain phrases and expressions to use when answering open-ended questions. Let's use a question from above: "In what ways does this family remind you of your own family?" Suppose a teacher asks this question after reading a story about a family, hoping students will talk about similarities and reasons and use phrases such as, "This family reminds me of my family because we have three children and sometimes we are hungry." Instead, a student says, "They have three childrens." You can help the student by providing a sentence starter. "This family reminds of me of my family because . . ." This scaffold enables English learners to stretch their language into longer sentences that make their logic explicit.

Some teachers put posters around the room that feature phrases and sentence starters that all students can use to extend their language. Putting up such posters isn't enough, of course. The posters will help only if you refer to them often. Here are some examples of posters that help students stretch their language.

To express an opinion:

- I think . . . because . . .

- I agree with . . . because . . .
- I disagree because . . .

To respond to readings and experiences:

- I was surprised to learn that . . .
- I wonder why . . .

To ask someone to clarify or elaborate:

- Could you say more about that?
- Could you give me an example of that?
- I don't understand. Can you tell me more?

To report what a classmate said:

- _____ said that . . .
- _____ thinks that . . .
- _____ wondered about . . .

Plan for Oral Presentations

In the culminating phase of inquiry-based learning, students plan for and present findings from their experiments to classmates and other audiences. This may be the most exciting part of the inquiry process. In this phase, students who have worked together to figure out ways to solve a challenge get to share what they have learned. In doing so, they take ownership of their learning. For English learners, presentations are an opportunity to use their developing English with a wide audience, some of whom are unfamiliar and have not yet seen their work. At the same time, presentations may be quite scary for English learners because visual and interpersonal cues available to them in face-to-face interaction are reduced. Presentations are challenging, too, because they require extended language without interactional scaffolding from classmates or the teacher. That is, in a more formal presentation where a small group is "on stage," English learners can't rely on the help they usually get in conversations, when others ask for clarification or for a repeat of what was just said. Lastly, presentations may be difficult for English learners because during the final part of the presentation devoted to "questions and answers," audience members may ask unanticipated questions the student is not prepared for.

You can minimize these challenges by helping students become consciously aware of the phases of the inquiry process from start to finish so they can, in turn, make their activities explicit to others. Graphic organizers, charts, and artwork depicting sequences students went through will help them see and name the whole sequence of what they've been doing. Once students have a fairly good idea of the processes they used during their investigations, they are ready to work more extensively on figuring out how they are going to present what they did, what they learned, and what they still need to learn—all to an outside audience.

As students plan how and what to present, you should be encouraging them to look back over their learning notebooks, charts, questions, and findings. You can assign short brainstorming sessions at this stage, too. The object would be to think of ways to present (e.g., demonstrations, dramas, murals, handmade movies, oral reports accompanied by PowerPoint presentations, and so on), and then see which kind of presentation fits best with what was investigated and how it was investigated. For instance, a drama would not have captured what happened in the study on motion and design in Ernestina's and Rebecca's classrooms, but a talk with visual aids followed by a demonstration did.

Part of the plan for the presentation has to include what each member of the group will do. Again, because the groups have been created strategically to include multiple student abilities and diverse language proficiencies, English learners are positioned favorably to take on roles that are both stretching yet also relatively safe. You might be tempted to allow the most capable students to take over the presentation and field all the questions from the audience (presenting and responding "on behalf of the total group"). But a more appropriate and productive choice is to ensure that all students in each group have a specific role to play in both the presentation and any question-and-answer exchanges that follow. Examples of roles might include these: Reader, Chart Holder, Reporter, Explainer, Demonstrator, Summarizer, and Responder to Questions From the Audience. Often, giving English learners a specific role to play, and ensuring they understand what they are expected to do, creates an emotionally safe zone in which they can produce language beyond what they may be capable of in more spontaneous situations. Moreover, if English learners know they have a role that involves saying something, they can rehearse and practice prior to the actual presentation. It is a good idea, therefore, to include time for rehearsals in your own teaching plans. Rehearsal provides a safe way for English learners to practice the oral and written language they will rely on during the presentation. Group members can help English learners with pronunciation and oral reading.

Planning for the presentation is also a time that favors trying out new vocabulary—specialized and precise words—to use during the presentation. One of the goals of inquiry learning is to have students "pick up" and use vocabulary that is specific to the topics and content areas they are studying. For example, in the inquiry science unit Ernestina and Rebecca were using, students were expected to use appropriately such words as *velocity, friction, motion,* and *force.* In other areas of study, such as literature, students might be expected to use words and expressions such as *theme, perspective, voice,* and *tone.* In a social studies inquiry about settlements, students might be required to talk about *boundaries, land grants, treaties,* and *resettlement.* Each area of study has its own set of specialized vocabulary and ways to use it. Focusing on specialized inquiry-topic vocabulary during the time when small groups are planning their presentations gives English learners an extra shot at hearing and using the new words. It also makes it more likely that students will incorporate that vocabulary into their presentations and into their responses during the follow-up question-and-answer time.

Keep Learning, Help Others

While this chapter presents many strategies and practices for SUPPORTING English learners and STRETCHING their language, there are, as you can imagine, many more for you to learn and try out. As you do that, we hope you'll be an ambassador for inquiry-based teaching. We hope you'll help others—teachers, community members, and school administrators—understand how such teaching has the potential to help English learners (as well as their English-proficient peers) gain greater access to subject matter, participate more fully, engage more deeply with ideas—in short, to thrive in an academic setting. We emphasize "potential" because, to return to what we've been talking about throughout this chapter, for English learners, inquiry-based teaching (actually, teaching based on any curricular approach) is not enough. English learners need you to SUPPORT them and to STRETCH their language.

CHAPTER 3

Literacy and Inquiry

Children who are presented with knowledge from the top down, as a body of facts to be memorized, accepted, and later evaluated, will never know how to question, how to look critically at an issue to see who benefits from their knowing the information. Indeed, they may never *learn how to learn*. In an inquiry-based classroom, knowledge has to get down off its throne and play nice. Information is understood to be pliable, capable of being shaped to new purposes.

Randy Bomer & Katherine Bomer,
For a Better World: Reading and Writing for Social Action

Are you getting a feel for why students love inquiry? Do you see how it connects kids and content and makes learning fun? If so, you'll be glad to know there's yet another exciting component to inquiry. To recognize it, you need to step back and watch kids engaged in inquiry. As you scan the classroom, do you notice kids reading and writing without a word of encouragement from the teacher? These students, who normally groan when directed to read and write, are immersed in written texts, sharing books with other students, and taking notes about ideas related to their inquiry questions. If you look closely, you can even see the many ways kids are using reading and writing while engaged in their inquiry projects. One group of students is reading a text and creating a timeline to make sense of what they are reading. Another group is creating signs (e.g., "Do Not Touch: Wet Paint") to remind classmates to keep their hands off. One student is skimming the pages of a phone book for the number of a geologist he wants to interview. Another student, over in the corner, is making a list of materials and books she needs to create a terrarium. In each case, kids are reading and writing in the service of learning. And herein lies that second exciting component of inquiry: literacy. Within an inquiry framework, students draw on reading and writing to supplement and extend their understandings of their topics and their world.

The Roles of Literacy in Inquiry-Based Curriculum

A simple way to figure out the roles literacy might play in an inquiry project is to ask yourself the following questions: What discipline best informs this inquiry? How do specialists in this discipline use reading and writing to inform their thinking and to organize their understandings? For example, in the Motion and Design unit, Ernestina and Rebecca knew they could learn more about the roles literacy could play in kids' learning by talking to an automotive engineer. They knew they would have to introduce students to the social activities related to design and motion, including observing, describing, comparing, and classifying—and writing down observations, descriptions, comparisons, and classifications.

Thinking about how specialists might use literacy as they work in their disciplines is one way to think about how you can make literacy a taken-for-granted part of any inquiry. Another is to think of the four roles for literacy we've listed below and how they can help promote any of the inquiry elements from Chapter 1.

- Literacy Promotes Wonderings
- Literacy Builds Background Knowledge
- Literacy Challenges, Clarifies, and Extends Knowledge
- Literacy Brings It All Together

Literacy Promotes Wonderings

The world is full of wonders. Kids naturally gravitate toward objects, noise, and smells that pique their curiosities. But inside the classroom, it isn't always easy to engage kids in what could intrigue them if only they'd attend to it. That is why we sometimes turn to forms of literacy and the vicarious experiences they provide to draw kids in and create a desire to learn more about a topic.

Reading Aloud to Students

Beautifully written and illustrated fiction and nonfiction books for children—and there are so many available—can spark our own imaginations about how to hook kids and provoke their wonderings. For example, if you want students to explore the Civil Rights movement, you could gather several books on the topic and read them aloud over three or four days, and then invite students to share what they noticed, what they thought, and what they wondered about as you were reading (see Figure 3.1).

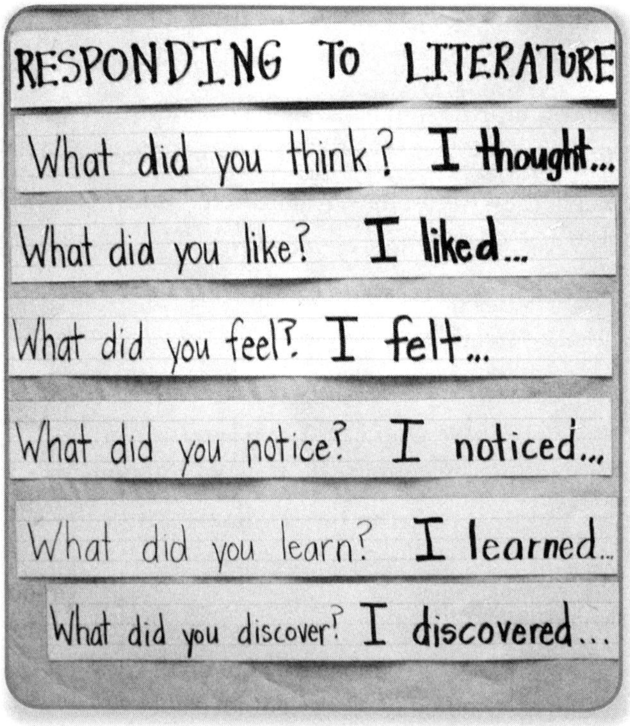

RESPONDING TO LITERATURE

What did you think? I thought...

What did you like? I liked...

What did you feel? I felt...

What did you notice? I noticed...

What did you learn? I learned...

What did you discover? I discovered...

Figure 3.1: **Inquiry Response Chart**

From *School Talk*, "Grand Conversations Across Texts" (2008) by K. Smith, S. Diaz & S. Edgerton

If these books included *Freedom on the Menu: The Greensboro Sit-Ins* (Weatherford, 2005), *Freedom School, Yes!* (Littlesugar, 2001), and *Grandmama's Pride* (Birtha, 2005), you might expect students to raise questions about nonviolent resistance, voting rights, and discriminatory public facilities and housing practices. On the other hand, if you were interested in a study of the environment, you might read several books from the Green Earth award winners (Web site: http://faculty.salisbury.edu/~elbond/greenactiv.html). Any of these books about the environment can inspire, inform, and pique students' curiosity about being good stewards of their world.

Picture Walks

Illustrations in children's picture books are integral to the story, so when students are invited to view illustrations before reading a book, they can anticipate a book's story line and vocabulary, and they can pose questions about what the illustrations make them think or wonder about. Teachers often guide students through this process using a picture walk accompanied by the STW discussion strategy (Anderson & Richards, 2003). You begin a picture walk by showing the students the book's cover, and then inviting them to look through the text, page by page, using the STW questions—*What Do I See? What Do I Think?* and *What Do I Wonder?*—to guide the discussion. At the conclusion of a picture walk, you have a sense of what students know about a topic and what language they possess to talk about it. Students usually enjoy the experience and are eager to read the book, or have it read to them, to find out what really happens.

The STW strategy moves children beyond simply reporting what they see to consider what the illustration makes them think and wonder about. For example, when viewing the cover of *This Is the Dream* (Shore & Alexander, 2006), shown in Figure 3.2, a student reported seeing a boy and a girl with a crowd behind them, but when asked to share what the illustration made him *think* about, he responded with, "I think they are in a dangerous place because there is a man with a helmet on standing behind them." Asked about what it made them *wonder*, another student said, "I wonder whose flag they are carrying? It's not the same as we have [the flag in our classroom]."

· · · Figure 3.2: **Cover of a picture book used for a picture walk**

*Picture Walks in the Students' Home Language*s

In cases where the students in class all speak the same non-English language (for instance, Spanish), you can conduct the picture walk in that language. If there are students in the class who speak and understand only English, the experience will be valuable to them as well. Moreover, previewing information or a story in another language positions students who speak that language as proficient language users, and it shows all students that other languages are meaningful. Many of Casey Bilger's third-grade students relied on their first language, Spanish, to discuss the pictures from *Harvesting Hope* (Krull, 2003), a biography of Cesar Chavez, as Casey displayed the pictures on a large screen for the students' responses. (See the Extra Clips section of the DVD for a demonstration of Casey and the students engaged in a picture walk of *Harvesting Hope*.)

Reader Response Logs

Reader response logs are used to record students' responses and reactions to readings. Sometimes, students keep individual logs of their own responses; sometimes, the teacher compiles students' responses on large chart paper. For the purpose of inquiry, you might ask students to respond first by sharing their initial reactions to the text, and then have them record what the text made them wonder about or want to know more about. When students' wonderings are collected over several readings around the same topic, you are able to generate long lists of questions. These questions can be categorized to focus a formal inquiry. One year, Karen Smith read aloud several books about the Japanese internment to a class of fifth graders and had them record their wonderings after each reading. A sample of their wonderings included:

> *Whose idea was it to intern the Japanese Americans?*
>
> *Where were the camps located?*
>
> *Did any of the internees escape?*
>
> *What happened to the houses they left behind?*
>
> *Why did the government wait so long to apologize?*
>
> *What were the barracks like to live in when it was cold outside?*
>
> *How did this experience compare to the Nazi-German experience?*
>
> *Why didn't the government intern Germans, or did they?*
>
> *What do Japanese social studies books say about the internment?*

After three days of reading and talking, the students wanted to study more about the internment, so Karen collected their response logs, compiled their questions on a single sheet of paper, and gave a copy to each student. Small groups of students then categorized the questions (e.g., comparing German and Italian concentration camps with Japanese internment camps in the U.S.; describing the circumstances under which Japanese Americans were removed from their homes and cities; investigating the daily lives of inmates of the Japanese internment camps; exploring the legal justification for instituting the Japanese camps and for discontinuing them), and each small group selected a category to explore over the following two weeks.

Literacy Builds Background Knowledge

As teachers, we know the importance of tapping into and building on students' prior knowledge to make learning relevant and meaningful. This is especially important when we begin an in-depth inquiry into topics with which students have limited experience and know little about. Spending a few days providing students with academically enriching experiences familiarizes them with the content. It also allows you to assess what they know about the topic, clarify their misconceptions, and determine how best to structure the focused unit of study. In the Motion and Design challenge, Ernestina and Rebecca developed students' understanding of physics concepts, such as speed, force, and acceleration, by engaging them in hands-on experiences. They also introduced students to literacy experiences that expanded their prior knowledge about the topic and helped them make accurate recordings of what they observed and then organized these data. Such literacy experiences were not unlike what engineers might do if they were charged with designing, constructing, and testing a vehicle to a set of specifications.

In work that builds background, your students will read and discuss a wide range of materials from photographs and movies, texts, sticky notes, and graphic organizers, and they'll be writing to learn, record, and explain new understandings. In Chapter 1, we shared the *Writing to Learn* graphic organizer that Ernestina and Rebecca used to organize their students' inquiries. Here we provide other literacy practices and scaffolds that help students build background knowledge.

Graphic Organizers

A good way to help your students read for an inquiry project is to use a graphic organizer, a visual organization of meaning based on students' understandings and suggestions. This can be done with a whole class, or with a small group of students working side by side. Typical graphic organizers are semantic webs, Venn diagrams, and tree diagrams.

Semantic Webs

To create a semantic web, you ask students to recall and brainstorm what they know about particular words or topics. Typically, students will produce words and comments that reflect diverse categories and levels of generalization. You write the words and ideas students generate exactly as they say them. Once you feel the students have given sufficient examples, you can go over the words and help students read the words they have generated. Next, you can work with the students to reorganize these into chunks of ideas that go together. This helps students develop connections among words and ideas, and in doing so, prepares them for subsequent readings and discussions that build their background knowledge.

Venn Diagrams

The Venn diagram is another type of graphic organizer. It is made up of overlapping circles and is used to examine similarities and differences in two or more items. It also helps students organize their thoughts about their topic. Students can easily make their own Venn diagrams using the following Web site: www.readwritethink.org/materials/venn/index.html. For example, when building background on the Civil Rights movement, students might read biographical texts about people such as Rosa Parks and Martin Luther King, Jr., who knew firsthand what life for African Americans was like during this period. After they read the texts, students could create a Venn diagram, noting how the two individuals' backgrounds, challenges, and/or accomplishments were similar and how they were different. (See Figure 3.3).

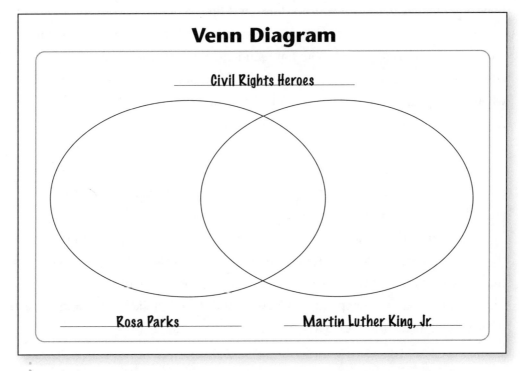

Figure 3.3: **Venn Diagram comparing Rosa Parks to Martin Luther King, Jr.**

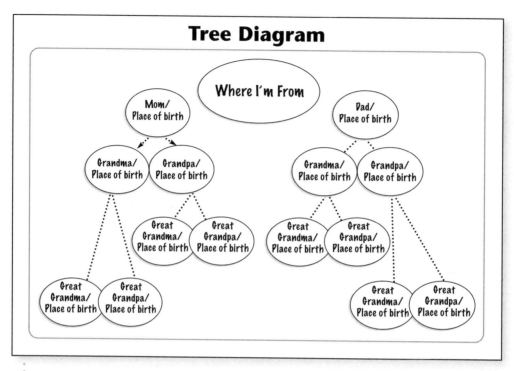

Figure 3.4: **Tree Diagram of Family Ancestors**

Tree Diagrams and Timelines

For content areas that involve procedures and time sequences, you can have students use tree diagrams or timelines to organize information into a possible sequence. In this manner, you can have students identify key vocabulary the author used to signal sequence. These forms of organizers support students when reading texts that involve temporal sequences, such as historical narratives, story narratives, trial-and-error sequences, and research experiments. They also help them plan for their own writing when they are authoring similar texts. During a unit on immigration, you might ask students to create a family tree using a tree diagram to track who their ancestors are and where they came from (see Figure 3.4).

Or, if students are comparing what was happening in Europe and in the Pacific during World War II, they could create a timeline, noting events that were occurring at the same time in history with one side of the line representing what was happening in Europe and the other side representing what was happening in the Pacific.

Predict From Photographs, Drawings, and Illustrations

To help with reading images, you can give students time in pairs or small groups to say what they think a particular photograph, drawing, or illustration is about. For example, using the image shown in Figure 3.5, students can pair off and discuss what they think the painting is about.

••• Figure 3.5: **Reading Images**
NWCLB® by Christian Faltis

There will be much in the discussion of this painting that can help build background for studies of immigration or segregation. Experiences in reading images and discussing the interpretations can pave the way for subsequent readings of print text.

Literacy Challenges, Clarifies, and Extends Knowledge

Once students have tapped into and extended their background knowledge on a topic, they are much better prepared for more extensive reading and writing experiences. As a reminder, in inquiry studies, we do not encourage kids to read and write for literacy's sake. Instead, we want them to engage in hands-on experiences that let them experience phenomena firsthand, and engage with primary sources such as science experiments, or artifacts such as letters, diaries, photographs, and maps that provide authentic materials from the past. However, along with these activities and texts, we do encourage further research using secondary sources such as texts, movies, and pictures to confirm or challenge their developing ideas. Here are some literacy practices you and your students can use to do this.

Maintain Reading Focus

You can scaffold reading texts with the RPM strategy: *Recall-Predict-Move On*. In this case, you ask students to recall any other texts, images, or discussions that might be relevant to the current reading. You may have to recall some of the background-building work you completed earlier in the study, if they don't bring it up in the discussion. You can then ask students to predict what might happen next, or what they predict the text will be about and how it will turn out. If appropriate, you can also ask them what sequence the story or information is likely to follow. Then, you move on, keeping in mind what students have predicted and their comments about the text.

Skim and Scan Texts and Images

When students skim a text or an image, the goal is to read it quickly to get a big picture of the content so that they have a general notion about what is being covered. You can help your students learn to skim by having them survey the selection's title, by looking over chapter headings and subheadings, by examining charts, tables, or pictures, and by reading and recording any individual words or blocks of texts they are unsure of or find interesting. The goal of scanning is to help students learn to predict what the passage is about based on the available supports being scanned. For inquiry reading, you might ask your students to *quickly* scan a text they think they want to use for their inquiry topic. You can explain to them that the purpose of scanning is to get a general idea about the material and decide if it is likely to contain information they are seeking.

Students can also scan lists of items or steps in a procedure to look for particular information. It is likely that students will scan their notebooks and

Writing to Learn charts for key information. Learning to skim and scan is especially important for students who read one word at a time and for readers who see all words in a text as equally important.

Read Text and Images a Second Time

Students need to get into the habit of carefully rereading texts and images to check if they have understood key ideas and information. They should keep notes of words and phrases they particularly liked or did not understand. In pairs, they can discuss these words and phrases with their partners. There are certain strategies you can encourage your students to use when they are having difficulty understanding the meaning of particular words and phrases.

- Keep reading to see if the context helps in making sense of the word or phrase.
- Look back at what comes before the word or phrase to see if the context helps make sense of the word or phrase.
- If there are photographs, drawings, or illustrations, use them to help with meaning.
- Think about how the word or phrase is being used. Is it an action or an object, or does it describe an action or an object?
- Use a bilingual dictionary and, if possible, ask a bilingual partner about the meaning of the word or phrase.
- Make sure you understand how an image is being used. If it is a graphic organizer, make sure you notice all of the parts being emphasized.

Say Something (adapted from Short, Harste & Burke, 1996)

This strategy helps students construct meaning and monitor their understanding. It is conducted between two children, or between an adult and a child. The pair decides together the points in the text at which they plan to stop and "say something" about what they have read. (The teacher may encourage students who are having trouble comprehending to stop after every paragraph or two.) The pair reads to the point at which they have decided to stop and say something. "Saying something" might be one of the following:

- Making a personal connection to the text
- Connecting the text to other texts they have read
- Connecting the text to some social or global issue

- Asking questions about a part they don't understand
- Noting points of agreement or disagreement with the text
- Retelling what they remember

After a brief discussion, the pair continues this same process until the text is completed.

Lift the Level of Understanding

The idea here is to build on your students' contributions during discussions of shared readings when you are involved with them. Your goal is to extend or reshape students' contributions into broader issues to be addressed in the inquiry lesson. For example, if you and the students are reading about ways to increase the speed of their vehicles, you might ask them to consider the relationship between more speed and the need for increased energy or force. This discussion could then lead to a broader conversation on the limits of energy with respect to the need for faster vehicles. Another example of "lifting the level" is to "translate" a student's talk about a topic into more academic language. This entails crediting the student for the initial comment while re-stating it in a more academic style. With English learners, you can lift the level of a student's contribution that may be difficult to understand by rephrasing what was said into comprehensible language.

Summarize the Text

When students read texts to extend understandings about their inquiry project, they should be able to mention the most important points of what they read. Learning to summarize takes practice. What students typically do is to look for key details that might be related to their inquiry. But summarizing is not about details; it is about the big ideas that students need to be aware of as they build their knowledge of the inquiry topic. While it is not necessary to summarize every text students read, it is worthwhile to have students summarize their goals, the key ideas they are investigating, and their new understandings.

To help students summarize, you can have them try the following practices:

- Draw or write out main ideas in six sentences with no more than six words per sentence.
- In side-by-side pairs, retell the main ideas of a reading in one minute or less.

- Have small groups of students each come up with a sentence that best sums up the main idea of the reading. Share the sentences across groups.
- Ask students to suggest a short title for each paragraph they read.

Reflections on Learning: Entrance and Exit Slips

Students can use entrance and exit slips to reflect on what they know at the beginning of class and at the end of class. Entrance slips take only a few minutes of students' time. At the very beginning of class, students write for just a few minutes, describing what they already know and listing questions they have about the day's topic. These slips are collected and read anonymously as a way to begin the day's work. Exit slips, on the other hand, are completed at the end of class. They ask students to summarize what was learned or completed that day or to reflect on strategies they used to learn new material (Gere, 1985). These, too, are often completed in just a few minutes. Sometimes, however, you may want to create prompts to guide students' exiting reflections to get more specific information. For example, besides asking students to summarize what they learned or list questions they have about their topics, you can ask them to describe any problems they encountered and what they did to solve the problems. Sometimes these problems relate to the activity itself; for example, in the unit on Motion and Design, Rebecca's and Ernestina's students noted that the clock broke and they didn't have time to complete their experiment. Other times, problems arise within groups working together cooperatively. In each of these reflective experiences, students are given an opportunity to revisit what they learned, and teachers are given information about what students are (or are not) learning and what needs to be done to support future learning.

Observation and Learning Logs

Ernestina's and Rebecca's students were well versed in recording observations. When they experimented with the effect weight had on the movement of their vehicles, they learned to make predictions, record time accurately, and describe what they observed, as shown in Figure 3.6.

Logging observations also gives students opportunities to apply academic vocabulary related to their research topics. Ernestina's and Rebecca's students were confidently and comfortably using terms such as *prediction, centimeters, friction, force,* and *energy* by the time their Motion and Design study ended.

Testing the motion of a vehicle
carrying a load

Directions: Use your falling weight system, your standard vehicle, the wooden blocks, and washers to test how weight affects the movement of your vehicle. After completing the experiment, answer the questions.

Prediction: What do you think will happen to your vehicle when weight is added to it?

I think the car will go really slow because of the block

How many small washers does it take to move your vehicle with 2 blocks? 16

Cargo	Time (seconds)	Observations: Describe how your vehicle moved.
No blocks	0:01³⁷	The car went fast and didn't stop 'til it hit the bookend.
No blocks	0:01⁶³	It went fast and didn't stop.
1 block	0:04⁹¹	It went very slow but it didn't stop
1 block	0:03³⁵	It went kinda fast and stoped when it hit the bookend
2 blocks	0:04⁴⁷	It didn't stop and it didn't go slow.
2 blocks	0:05⁰⁶	It didn't go very fast.

Figure 3.6: **Observation Sheet**

Side-by-Side Learning

This was most notable in their final projects, in which they were required to provide a visual description of their vehicle, a written plan for how they conducted their final test, and an oral presentation of what they learned using academic terms to explain what they had learned.

Like observation logs, learning logs provide a place for students to record what they are learning. Writing helps us learn by assisting us in organizing what we are learning—facts, concepts, patterns—into meaningful knowledge. In Figure 3.7 below, the student used both documentation of his observation and his learning to make sense of and record what he was learning.

Many teachers find it beneficial to have students trade their observation and learning logs weekly with a peer for a response.

Gallery Walk (adapted from Manitoba Career Development, www.edu.gov.mb.ca/k12/cur/cardev/gr10_found/appendixb.pdf)

The gallery walk strategy is a good way for students to review the content they are learning and for the teacher to assess it. The process is fairly simple. You begin by setting up stations around the room based on various aspects of the

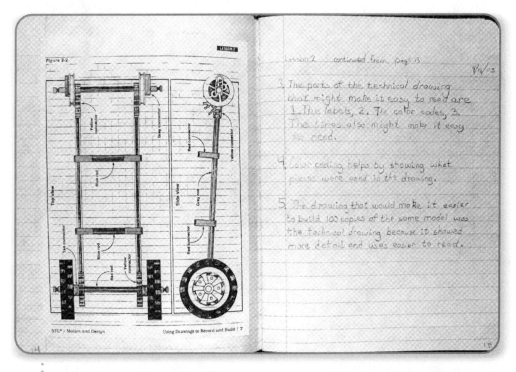

Figure 3.7: **Student's Science Log from Web site with unit on Design and Motion,** from www.ksd.org

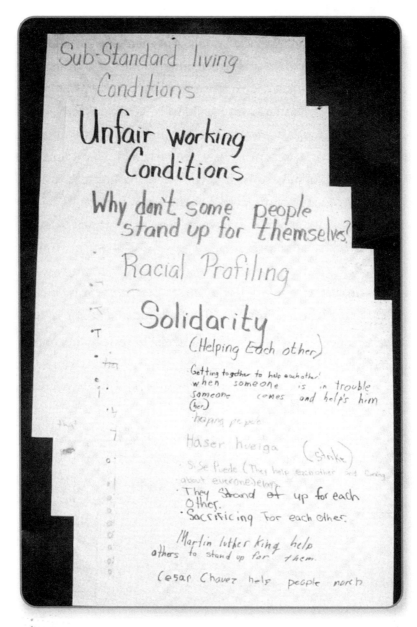

Figure 3.8: **Gallery Walk Chart**
From *School Talk*, "Grand Conversations Across Texts" by
K. Smith, S. Diaz, & S. Edgerton

Side-by-Side Learning

inquiry topic. Each station has a display of materials dealing with one aspect of the inquiry topic and an accompanying chart for students to record their responses to the display, or simply a chart headed by a focus question. (Be sure the charts are at eye level so students can read them easily.) In pairs or small groups, students visit the displays or charts, observing the displays, addressing the focus questions or topics, and responding to previous visitors' responses, if they were not the first group. One group member records responses and questions on the blank chart. After three or four minutes, students move to the next display or chart and repeat the same process. Once students have rotated through all the stations, each group returns to its original display or chart, reads through the responses, and creates a summary, which they share with the class. Silvia Edgerton's fifth-grade students participated in a gallery walk in the midst of their study of migrant life in the Southwest. As they moved from chart to chart, they responded with ideas and questions they had about major themes that had emerged throughout their study (see Figure 3.8).

Literacy Brings It All Together

In an inquiry-based curriculum, the goal in the final phase is twofold: the development of questions that continue to extend students' thinking, and their application of what they have learned through firsthand knowledge to create final projects to be shared with others. Often, these final projects require the use of various forms of literacy.

Create Graphics and Visuals

Your students can collaborate and share new understandings by filling in graphic organizers and making drawings, such as timelines, murals, and illustrations of key components in their inquiry. Students can also write out information related to their inquiry project and read it to others in small groups for discussion and clarification. In the Motion and Design unit, students created visuals to show how their vehicle looked at the start of the design and in its final form. They also created charts for focusing their presentations (see Figure 3.9).

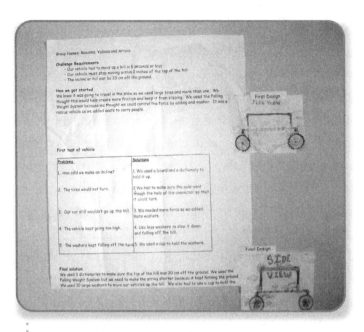

• • • Figure 3.9: **Final Presentation Poster**

This chart served two purposes: It caused students to reflect on and rethink what they had learned, and it provided a prompt for students who were less confident and competent using English during their final presentations.

Casey Bilger invited his third graders to create a mural that represented their new understandings about migrant life. The children also rehearsed what they wanted to say about the part of the mural they created. This rehearsal prepared them for the public presentation they made to their classmates and a group of fifth-grade students. (Go to the Extra Clips section of the DVD to see the mural the students created and to view one student's final presentation.)

Use Mentor Texts to Structure Presentations

Do your students dread the traditional research report that is often required when they research a topic for a school assignment? One reason this assignment may be so disliked is that its form is often pre-designed and lacks the individual student's writing style and voice. One way to honor the value of written reports yet make them personal is to engage students in a genre study of the structure of reports. A genre study of reports would be conducted during writing workshop. It is in writing workshop that genres, such as memoir, fiction, mysteries, literary nonfiction, and so on, are studied. The mode of study, even in writing workshop, is—no surprise—inquiry. Genre studies during writing workshop can focus on text structures as complex as a report, or texts that provide visual displays or organize observations. The following framework for studying how a genre is structured was developed by Isoke Nia (1999).

Unit of Study Framework for Studying the Structure of Genres

Best-guess gathering: The students and teacher gather examples of the genre.

Immersion: Students and teacher immerse themselves in the examples and find those elements of sound and structure that seem to define the genre.

Sifting: After immersing themselves in the examples for three or four days, students select those examples that are the best models for their definition of the genre and that they feel will support them as they carry the study forward.

Second immersion: Students immerse themselves in the examples they identified in the sifting as the best models for this study. They pay close attention to details in the authors' writing and they identify a touchstone text they will use to support their own writing in this genre.

Touchstone try-its: Students' inquiries are focused on how the text's author went about his/her writing. The students try out some of these moves in their own writing.

Writing: Students write throughout the study, collecting ideas in their logs or notebooks and trying out crafting techniques in their own writing. Ultimately, they draft, revise, edit, and publish or present a piece in the genre under study.

Reflecting and assessing: Students and the teacher spend time reflecting on and assessing both the processes and products of their writing experience within the unit of study.

NOTE: *Primary Voices K–6* (1999) explains this framework and includes several articles by teachers who used the framework to develop units of study on memoir, fiction, and other topics (e.g., Arnberg, 1999; Goldfarb, 1999; Angelillo, 1999; Reduce, 1999).

Situated Academic Discourse

We would feel remiss if we didn't say a few words about situated academic discourse because it is so important to students' learning. All disciplines have their own sets of values, worldviews, ways of acting, and ways of talking and writing (Gee, 1990). Therefore, when students begin an investigation into a topic, their activity requires more than carrying out experiments and discussing primary sources of data. It also requires learning to talk and act and see and value in specialized ways that are part of the discipline itself. Such learning happens through taking on, even if temporarily and tentatively, the identity of being a member of that discipline. For example, in the optimal case, students who conduct an inquiry of the history of their communities become historians, assembling historical artifacts as historians do, questioning the connections among the artifacts as historians do, posing and testing their own theories as historians do.

It is our job to make sure students learn the tools of the discipline they are investigating as well as the facts about their topics. And the best way to do that is to make it easy for students to take on the identity of those who are in the discipline working with those topics. Ernestina and Rebecca provide a clear picture for how to achieve this goal—a hybrid of immersion, instruction, and curriculum arranging. They immersed their students in the job of automotive engineers, connecting new language that went with that discipline to activity required by the discipline. They instructed by using everyday language to introduce new vocabulary and concepts to students as they carried out their work as engineers. And they used the specialized language of design and motion while, throughout the study, they arranged the curriculum so that students had multiple opportunities to try out and apply this language in the context of real use. This continuous exposure and use resulted in all students taking up the academic discourse of automotive engineers.

The Teacher's Role

It probably goes without saying that the teacher plays a significant role in helping students determine ways language and literacy can support their investigations. It's important for teachers to be aware of how literacy and language function within specific discourse communities. Equally important is introducing and demonstrating these practices at opportune moments when kids need them. Ernestina and Rebecca often introduced new ways of recording information to the whole class right at the point kids would find them useful and could apply them. For example, when kids began testing their vehicles to control speed, the teachers created a large observation form on chart paper, so all the students could see it. They demonstrated both the activity (e.g., how to slow down a vehicle by adding weight to it) and ways to record it. Students were then given the same form to use as they ran multiple tests to determine the effect of weight on their vehicle's movement. As students tried out recording data, and using oral and written academic language as they recorded their observations, Ernestina and Rebecca circulated among them and helped them with their attempts to use the observation form and their newly acquired language. Students' attempts were treated as approximations, but with several opportunities to practice these specialized ways of talking, reading, and writing, students eventually appropriated them and made them their own. In other words, a focus on learning about designing a vehicle that moved according to particular specifications, coupled with reading and writing in the service of designing that vehicle, enhanced students' literacy.

CHAPTER 4

Turn, Turn, Turn: Challenging "The Way Things Are"

A democracy depends on public attention to the concerns of its members. . . . If the voices of the vulnerable are silent, there is no hope of renewal or justice.

Randy Bomer & Katherine Bomer,
For a Better World: Reading and Writing for Social Action

We've been saying throughout this book that you don't have to march straight through a commercial program or a teacher's manual. You can sashay. It's true: mandates put limits on what you do. They tie your hands—sometimes all the way up to your elbows. But it's possible to wiggle free a little (or a lot) and adapt almost any curriculum so that kids of varying abilities with English can all learn together, side by side. You can even enrich scripted programs if you have any room at all to maneuver. Katharine Johnson (Edelsky & Johnson, 2004) carved out a "talk-back" time for her second graders to critique their required reading programs and rebut what they saw as unfair depictions of minorities.

The curriculum we've been advocating throughout this book is a turn toward inquiry. As we've been saying, inquiry—open-ended and lending itself to small-group work—is a boon for English learners and English speakers together. More than that, inquiry has significant advantages for learning. It engages students in using the tools of a discipline (e.g., the tool of standard experimental procedures in science, the tool of original sources in history). It integrates different disciplines (such as physics and math, or biology, history, and art). It promotes what is often referred to as "higher-order thinking" (synthesizing, interpreting, analyzing, evaluating). It encourages kids to use literacy authentically (for remembering, documenting, planning, reporting) and to talk to one another using academic language (a boon for learning English). And it promotes an inquiry stance toward learning in general—curiosity and a willingness to sustain an interest, to get beneath the surface facts, and to remain open to new information.

To show how you can turn curriculum toward inquiry, we used examples from a science unit. But, as you read in Chapter 1, you can foreground students' questions and wonderings no matter what the content. In literacy, for instance, what do kids wonder about in lessons in a mandated spelling program? What questions do they have about spelling as they look at historical documents? How do authors of mysteries give readers clues? What makes memoir different from autobiography? Kids can gather data in any area— school subjects or not (e.g., they can observe and record which items packed in school lunches from home have a higher trading value). New learnings can be presented at the end of any unit of study. All of these elements of inquiry (questioning, experimenting, collecting and analyzing data, presenting what's been learned) can turn a packaged curriculum into one that is more engaging, more likely to require authentic literacy and language use, and more welcoming for students with a range of abilities in English.

A Critical Turn

There's yet another way to deepen and enrich the curriculum: Give it a critical turn. Taking a critical turn means questioning what is taken for granted, trying to find out how things got to be the way they are, figuring out whose "story" it is—whose perspective is presented as "just the way things are," and whose perspective is missing, always asking such questions against a yardstick of justice and equity. Questioning "the way things are" might mean looking into how and when wearing designer clothing became important to youngsters. Trying to find out how things got to be the way they are could mean tracking down exactly when and how young children began to know brand names of jeans, sneakers, T-shirts, and sunglasses. Putting concerns for justice and equity at the forefront of the study might entail investigating the details of who benefits from creating concerns among children about brands of clothing.

It is possible to turn curriculum critical by doing something as relatively simple as questioning common sense. For example, in a unit on weather, you can question the common sense that weather just happens; in a unit on human prehistory, you can interrogate (think of police interrogations or of a dog gnawing a bone) the common sense that race is biologically real. For instance, who believes that race is biological and who doesn't? Whose views prevail about race? What resources are available to whom for promoting their views on race? What struggles have occurred/are occurring over how to think about race (or weather, or any other topic)? This last question about struggles over different perspectives is a good one for turning just about any topic critical. Asking questions about other perspectives on a topic, other voices, other stories about slaves, about the "westward movement," about union organizing or community helpers or immigration, lets kids try to find out who holds those views, who tells those stories, and what outlets are available for telling each one.

Although this book is about turning curriculum toward inquiry, we actually think the critical turn is ultimately more important. For one thing, a critical turn requires inquiry. (The reverse is not true; inquiry-based teaching is not necessarily critical.) Because critical teaching (known variously as critical curriculum, critical literacy, critical pedagogy) questions what is assumed to be "neutral" knowledge or even "common sense," the answers to critical questions are not always known—or at least they are not readily available (after all, what school textbook gets beneath the "facts" of the settling of the West to reveal the way this period is seen by Native Americans?). A critical turn, therefore, provides all the benefits of inquiry—encouraging students to really want to get to the bottom of something; to be eager (not merely willing) to keep on digging and poking around; to hunt for original documents, firsthand information, and informants (akin to finding eyewitnesses); to pursue leads and retrace steps when caught in dead ends; to assemble bits of the puzzle from data collected from a variety of sources until a bigger picture begins to come into focus. All of this entails using literacy for authentic communicative purposes and offering ways for all students to participate, both of which support English learning and literacy learning.

But a critical turn does still more. When you turn the curriculum toward the critical, you provide the kind of education needed for democracy.

Education is not only for preparing workers; it is also for developing citizens. It is for promoting habits of mind (questioning, reasoning, evaluating) and heart (caring about the general good) for civic participation. When you teach with a critical turn, you make certain principles familiar—principles of justice and equity, principles needed now more than ever as the public tunes out information about the intensifying gap between rich and poor (along with the shrinking of the middle), as corporate and government scandals have to become more and more outrageous to warrant more than one day's worth of headlines.

Right now you're probably asking why, if a critical turn is so superior, this entire book and DVD aren't about just that. The fact is, we wanted them to be. But maybe because of the limitations in our own understandings of physics (remember we said at the outset that the topic Rebecca and Ernestina were dealing with was not at all our area of expertise), we couldn't imagine a critical turn in a mandated unit on motion and design in physics. If the unit had been in the social studies or language arts or even the biological sciences, we'd have been up to the task, and so would have Rebecca and Ernestina. They could have turned topics in any of these fields into investigations with a critical edge.

As it is, they took the topic of simple force, motion, and design—a topic accompanied by mandated packaged materials—and did a remarkable job of turning that into an inquiry. We're suggesting that you can do that, too.

We'd like to leave you with both a challenge and an opening. If literacy instruction mandates are limiting you, break free with inquiry into content. If you can't take on a full inquiry stance, infuse inquiry elements. If you can't infuse a lot of them, try a few. One is better than none. If you can envision inquiry in your classroom, try imagining a critical turn. If you can't do that throughout the year because the content doesn't lend itself easily to critical questions (e.g., a physics unit on force, motion, and design), try that turn with merely a couple of units of study. Or one. Or try just a little bit of a turn. Then another. Soon you'll be dancing!

Appendix: Forms and Charts

Writing to Learn

Source:

Facts:

Response:

Connections:

I wonder:

I want to know:

Source:

Facts:

Response:

Connections:

Now that I know ——————

I'm interested in knowing ——————

——————

——————

——————

Side-by-Side Learning: Exemplary Literacy Practices for English Language Learners and English Speakers in the Mainstream Classroom © 2008 by Carole Edelsky, Karen Smith, and Christian Faltis, Scholastic Professional
From Yellow Brick Roads: Shared and Guided Paths to Independent Reading 4–12 by Janet Allen, copyright © 2000, reprinted with permission of Stenhouse Publishers.

B-K-W-L-Q

Build Background	What Do I Know?	What Do I Want to Know?	What Did I Learn?	What New Questions Do I Have?

Side-by-Side Learning: Exemplary Literacy Practices for English Language Learners and English Speakers in the Mainstream Classroom © 2008 by Carole Edelsky, Karen Smith, and Christian Faltis, Scholastic Professional

From *Yellow Brick Roads: Shared and Guided Paths to Independent Reading 4–12* by Janet Allen, copyright © 2000, reprinted with permission of Stenhouse Publishers.

Categories of Questions

Yes/No Questions, Specific	Vague Questions	Unanswerable Questions	Not Doable Questions	Doable, Answerable Questions With Information

Side-by-Side Learning: Exemplary Literacy Practices for English Language Learners and English Speakers in the Mainstream Classroom © 2008 by Carole Edelsky, Karen Smith, and Christian Faltis, Scholastic Professional

Bookmarks

Response Prompts

Excuse me . . .

I'd like to add to what you just said . . .

I disagree because . . .

I agree because . . .

I don't understand what you mean . . .

I'm confused about . . .

Discussion Prompts

I liked _____ because . . .

I felt _____ because . . .

I thought _____ because . . .

I wish _____ because . . .

I was surprised by _____ because . . .

Side-by-Side Learning: Exemplary Literacy Practices for English Language Learners and English Speakers in the Mainstream Classroom
© 2008 by Carole Edelsky, Karen Smith, and Christian Faltis, Scholastic Professional

Inquiry-Based Assessment

Name _____ Date _____

PROCESS	COMMENTS
Uses appropriate methods for gathering data (e.g., writing letters, interviewing, experimenting, observing, reading, etc.)	
Formulates good questions	
Spends time reading, writing, observing, reflecting, etc.	
Asks good questions	
Explains, demonstrates, helps others	
Plans, organizes, and carries through on tasks	
Understands new ideas	

ATTITUDE	COMMENTS
Is willing to be challenged	
Is productive during work time	
Contributes willingly to group work	
Displays sensitivity and respect for others	
Learns from watching and working with others	

PRODUCT	COMMENTS
Is well developed and organized	
Is visually pleasing	
Provides detail	
Communicates effectively what student has learned	

PRESENTATION	COMMENTS
Articulates and/or demonstrates ideas clearly	
Is well informed	
Handles questions with authority and control	
Gives good examples	

Adapted from Reimer, Stephens, & Smith, 1993. *Side-by-Side Learning: Exemplary Literacy Practices for English Language Learners and English Speakers in the Mainstream Classroom* © 2008 by Carole Edelsky, Karen Smith, and Christian Faltis, Scholastic Professional

Venn Diagram

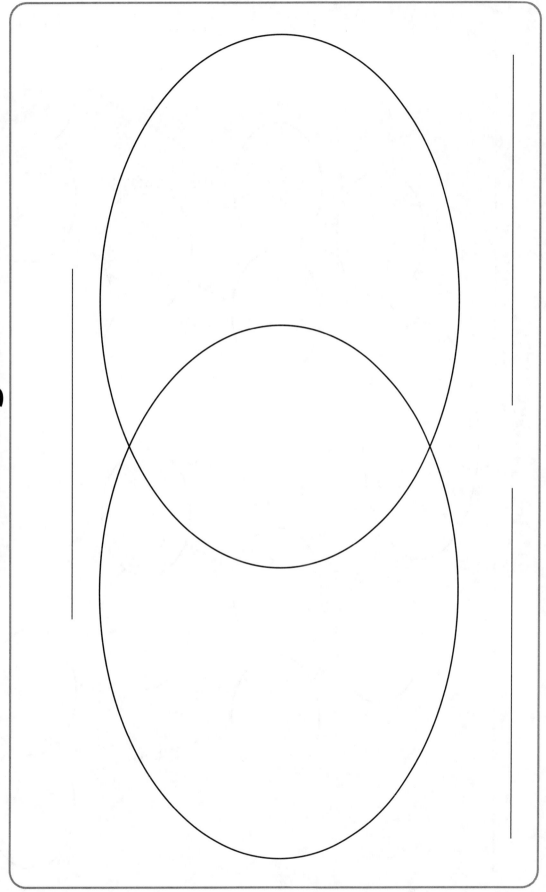

Side-by-Side Learning: Exemplary Literacy Practices for English Language Learners and English Speakers in the Mainstream Classroom © 2008 by Carole Edelsky, Karen Smith, and Christian Faltis, Scholastic Professional

Tree Diagram

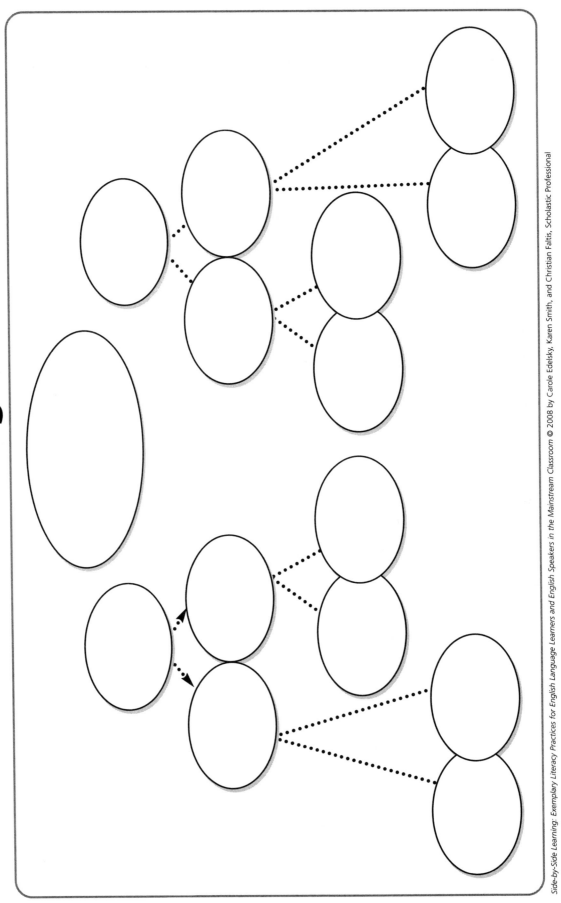

Side-by-Side Learning

Side-by-Side Learning: Exemplary Literacy Practices for English Language Learners and English Speakers in the Mainstream Classroom © 2008 by Carole Edelsky, Karen Smith, and Christian Faltis, Scholastic Professional

Entrance and Exit Slips

Entrance Slip

Name _____ Date _____

_____

_____

_____

_____

_____

_____

Exit Slip

Name _____ Date _____

_____

_____

_____

_____

_____

_____

Side-by-Side Learning: Exemplary Literacy Practices for English Language Learners and English Speakers in the Mainstream Classroom
© 2008 by Carole Edelsky, Karen Smith, and Christian Faltis, Scholastic Professional

Inquiry Daily Planning

Date _____

Inquiry Question:

Plan for the Day:

1.

2.

3.

4.

Materials and Resources Needed:

Team Members:

Accomplishments:

Side-by-Side Learning: Exemplary Literacy Practices for English Language Learners and English Speakers in the Mainstream Classroom
© 2008 by Carole Edelsky, Karen Smith, and Christian Faltis, Scholastic Professional

References

Allen, J. (2000). *Yellow brick roads: Shared and guided paths to independent reading 4–12.* Portland, ME: Stenhouse Publishers.

Anderson, N. A., & Richards, J. C. (2003). What do I see? What do I think? What do I wonder? (STW): A visual literacy strategy to help emergent readers focus on storybook illustrations. *The Reading Teacher,* 56(5), 442–443.

Angelillo, J. (1999). Using the writer's notebook across the day and beyond the writing workshop. *Primary Voices K–6,* 8(1), 30–36.

Arnberg, A. (1999). A study of memoir. *Primary Voices K–6,* 8(1), 13–21.

Callison, D. (1999). Key words in instruction: Inquiry. *School Library Media Activities Monthly,* XV(6), 38–42.

Edelsky, C., & Johnson, K. (2004). Critical whole language practice in time and place. *Critical Inquiry in Language Studies,* 1, 121–141.

Gee, J. (1990). *Social linguistics and literacies.* London: Falmer.

Gere, A. R. (1985). *Roots in the sawdust: Writing to learn across the disciplines.* Urbana, IL: National Council of Teachers of English.

Goldfarb, C. (1999). Ninja turtles, space aliens, and regular folks: A fifth-grade genre study of fiction. *Primary Voices K–6,* 8(1), 22–29.

Houghtaling, P. (Winter, 2003). The art of questioning. *Foxprint.* Retrieved February 7, 2007 from http://www.natureskills.com/art_of_questioning.html

National Science Resources Center. (2003). *Motion and Design* (Science and Technology for Children Books). Washington, DC: National Academies Press.

Nia, I. (1999). Units of study in the writing workshop. *Primary Voices K–6,* 8(1), 3–11.

Ogle, D. (1986). K-W-L: A teaching model that develops active reading of expository text. *Reading Teacher* 39 (6), 564–570.

Ray, K. W. (1999). *Wonderous Words.* Urbana, IL: National Council of Teachers of English.

Reduce, A.D. (1999). Genre study of non-fiction writing: Feature articles, editorials, and essays. *Primary Voices K–6,* 8(1), 33–44.

Reimer, K. M., Stephens, D., & Smith, K. (1993). Reflections. *Primary Voices K–6,* 1(1), 31.

Short, K. G., Harste, J., & Burke, C. (1996). *Creating classrooms for authors and inquirers* (2nd. ed.). Portsmouth, NH: Heinemann.

Smith, K., Diaz, S., & Edgerton, S. (2008). Grand conversations across texts: Making inquiry intentional and intertextual. *School Talk,* 13(3).

Children's Books

Birtha, B. (2005). *Grandmama's pride.* Morton Grove, IL: Albert Whitman & Company.

DiCamillo, K. (2003). *The Tale of Despereaux.* Cambridge, MA: Candlewick Press.

Krull, K. (2003). *Harvesting hope.* (Y. Morales, Ill.) New York: Harcourt.

Littlesugar, A. (2001). *Freedom school, yes!* (F. Cooper, Ill.) New York: Penguin Putnam.

Pfister, M. (1992). *The rainbow fish.* New York: North-South Books.

Shore, D., & Alexander, J. (2006). *This is the dream.* (J. Ransome, Ill.) New York: HarperCollins.

Weatherford, C. B. (2005). *Freedom on the menu: The Greensboro sit-ins* (J. Lagarrigue, Ill.) New York: Dial Books for Young Readers.

Walters, G. (Producer), & Stanton, A. (Writer/Director). (2003). *Finding Nemo* [Motion picture]. United States: Walt Disney Pictures.

Index

A

abilities, grouping students with mixed, 46–47

academic discourse, situated, 78

accommodations for English learners, problems with, 7–9

adaptations, inquiry-based, 9

Allen, Janet, *Yellow Brick Roads: Shared and Guided Paths to Independent Reading 4–12*, 25–26, 28

Anderson, N. A., and Richards, J. C., *Reading Teacher, The*, 61

Angelillo, J., *Using the writer's notebook across the day and beyond the writing workshop*, 77

Arnberg, A., *Study of memoir, A*, 77

assessment, as a part of good teaching, 36

B

B-K-W-L-Q graphic organizer, 25–26, 87

background knowledge, building, 12, 22, 24–27, 64–67

Baker, Tom, 31–32

Birtha, B., *Grandmama's Pride*, 61

Bomer, Randy, and Bomer, Katherine, *Better World, For a: Reading and Writing for Social Action*, 57, 80

Bookmarks, Response and Discussion Prompts form, 89

brainstorming, in collaborative writing, 50–51

C

Callison, Daniel, 18–20

Categories of Questions graphic organizer, 88

charts, using to support students, 42

controlled inquiry, 18–19

critical turn, taking a, 82–84

D

demonstrations, incorporating, 14, 44–45

design challenge, 32–36

DiCamillo, Kate, *Tale of Despereaux, The*, 6

dictation, taking, 43–44

drawings, predicting from, 67

DVD, side-by-side learning, 10–15

E

Edelsky, C., and Johnson, K., *Critical Inquiry in Language Studies*, 81

English as a second language (ESL) classrooms, 8

English learners and speakers, 5–9

Entrance and Exit Slips, 71, 93

experiential learning, 11

F

facial expressions, using to support English learners, 40–41

Finding Nemo, 19–20

foregrounding students' questions, 12, 22, 27–32

free inquiry, 20

G

Gallery Walk, 73–75

Gee, J., *Social Linguistics and Literacies*, 78

genres, framework for studying the structure of, 77

Gere, A.R., *Roots in the Sawdust: Writing to learn across the disciplines*, 71

gestures, using to support English learners, 40–41

Goldfarb, C., *Ninja turtles, space aliens, and regular folks: A fifth-grade genre study of fiction*, 77

Goudvis, Anne, *Ladybugs, Tornadoes, and Swirling Galaxies: English Language Learners Discover Their World Through Inquiry*, 38

graphic organizers, 64–67

graphics, creating, 75–76

groupings, 14

guided inquiry, 19

H

Houghtaling, Paul, "Art of Questioning, The," 30–32

I

illustrations, predicting from, 67

images, skimming and scanning, 68-69

inquiry and literacy. see literacy and inquiry

Inquiry Assessment form, 37, 90

inquiry-based curriculum, 9, 10–11

    approaches to, 18–20

    conditions that support, 21–22

    introduction, 16–18

    knowledge of processes and elements, 22–36

Inquiry Daily Planning form, 94

Inquiry Response chart, 60

K

K-W-L chart, 25, 27

Krull, K., *Harvesting Hope*, 62–63

L

language support, 13

learners, English, 5–9

learning literacy, support for, 15

learning, presenting new, 22, 33–36

level of understanding, lifting, 70

literacy and inquiry

    bringing it all together, 75–77

    building background knowledge, 64–67

    challenging, clarifying and extending knowledge, 67–75

    introduction, 57–58

    wonderings, promoting through literacy, 59–63

Littlesugar, A., *Freedom School, Yes!*, 61

logs, observation and learning, 71–73

M

Manitoba Career Development, 73–75

mentor texts, using to structure presentations, 76–77

modeled inquiry, 19–20

N

National Science Resources Center, *Motion and Design*, 34

Nia, Isoke, *Primary Voices K–6*, 77

O

Observation Sheet, 72

Ogle, D., Reading Teacher, 25

oral presentations, planning for, 54–56

P

"paraphrase passport," 46

participation, ensuring all students have access to, 45–46

Pfister, M., *Rainbow Fish, The*, 19–20

photographs, predicting from, 67

Picture Walks, 61–63

primary language, encouraging students to use their, 43

Q

questions. see also Categories of Questions graphic organizer

    categories of, 29–31

    strategies for asking, 31–32

    varying to students, 51–54

R

Ray, K. W., *Wonderous Words*, 24

Reader Response logs, 63

reading aloud to students, 59–61

reading focus, maintaining, 68

Reduce, A.D., *Genre study of non-fiction writing: Feature articles, editorials, and essays*, 77

Reimer, K. M., Stephens, D., and Smith, K., *Primary Voices K–6*, 37, 90

routines, 13

S

saying something, 69–70

second language learning, support for, 13–14

second time, reading text and images a, 69

Semantic Webs, 64–65

Shore, D., and Alexander, J., *This is the Dream*, 61

Short, K. G., Harste, J., and Burke, C., *Creating Classrooms for Authors and Inquirers*, 69–70

Smith, K., Diaz, S., and Edgerton, S., *School Talk*, 60, 74

speakers, English, 5–9

STRETCH Principle, the, 39, 47–56

study, focusing and conducting, 22, 32–33

STW discussion strategy, 61

support for second language learning

    introduction, 38–39

    STRETCH Principle, the, 47–56

    SUPPORT Principle, the, 39–47

T

teacher's role, the, 78–79

text, summarizing, 70–71

"think-pair-share," 46

topics, finding and investing in, 24–27

Tree Diagrams and Timelines, 66–67, 92

V

Van Sluys, Katie, *What If and Why: Literacy Invitations for Multilingual Classrooms*, 16

Venn Diagrams, 65, 91

visual aids, using to help English learners, 41

visuals, creating, 75-76

W

Walters, G. and Stanton, A., *Finding Nemo*, 77

Weatherford, C. B., *Freedom on the Menu: The Greensboro Sit-ins*, 61

wonderings, promoting through literacy, 59–63

writing

    collaborative, 50–51

    frequent informal, 48–50

Writing to Learn graphic organizer, 25–29, 86